CW00457563

Honeywell
'THE HAPPIEST STREET IN BARNSLEY'

Memories of life on and around the street

Honeywell Reminiscences Group

Publisher:
Williow Bank Community Partnership,'T.A.R.A' Office, Honeywell Community
Centre, Honeywell Street, Barnsley South Yorkshire. S71 1PH

Printed by:
Hot Metal Press, Elsecar Heritage Centre, Elsecar, Barnsley. S74 8HJ

ISBN No: 978-0-9570734-0-1

Vol. 1

2011

ACKNOWLEDGEMENTS

Willow Bank Community Partnership, and its members for providing funding and support for this project.

Thank you to everyone who has attended meetings; contributed stories and photographs, and helped us during our fundraising efforts.

Many thanks to those who have been involved in our working group who have given extra time and support as follows:

Gloria Hesford (Chair), Julie Johnson (Secretary), Elaine Jackson (Treasurer), Cllr. Bill Gaunt (Archivist), Laraine Day (Proof Reading), Katherine Symcox, Sid Williams, Doris Gosling and E. Phillips.

Andy Phillips, for the wonderful sketches in this book. (pages 16,32,52,62,115)

Stefan Boberek for adaptation of the front cover photograph.

Thank you to those who have given additional material for this book as follows:

Barnsley MBC's Archives and Local Studies Department

The Barnsley Chronicle

The Tasker Trust, for allowing us to use some of their wonderful photographs of Honeywell, from their own collection.

OS and Landmark Information Group for allowing us permission to use the Ordnance Survey Map of 1855 (Honey Well Colliery story).

Berneslei Homes for use of the Honeywell Community Centre.

Collating, transcribing and editing of stories and features:
Gloria Hesford and Julie Johnson

Proof reading:
Laraine Day and Julie Johnson

Collating and Catalogue of Photographs:
Gloria Hesford

Decisions on stories and photographs to be used:
Gloria Hesford, Julie Johnson and Elaine Jackson

Layout of Book:
Julie Johnson

Artwork within Book
Gloria Hesford

Book Design
Group Decisions

Contents

Foreword.

The credit for the book's original beginnings must go to "The Willow Bank Community Partnership" who wanted to do something for the community of Honeywell. Their idea was to collect stories and pictures from residents of the entire Honeywell area, both young and old, hopefully helping to draw the community back together. A group of interested people got together and the 'Honeywell Reminiscences Group' was born. We meet up on the last Saturday morning of the month at the Honeywell Community Centre, and anyone who cares to come along is made most welcome.

This book contains a collection of stories and pictures from our members, and although we as a group have evolved slightly from what was originally intended, we are pleased with the result. We have a fair size collection of photographs, far too many for this book, and we are sorry not to be able to include them all, but we have tried to put a good selection together. Future plans are being put forward for a second book; hopefully to include many more of the wonderful pictures we have been given. Sometimes photographs can say so much more than words.

Gloria Hesford

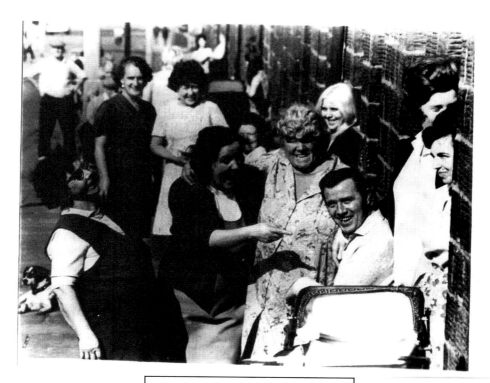

'The Happiest Street'
In Barnsley

Introduction

On behalf of the 'Honeywell Reminiscences Group,' we particularly want to thank the Willow Bank Community Partnership and all its members for providing us with the funds to bring this project to fruition.

When I first heard about the possibility of a book of people's memories being written about Honeywell, I couldn't wait to get started, although the story I wanted to tell was not so much mine but my dad's, Tommy Phillips, who was a true *'Honeyweller.'* He was born and raised on Honeywell Street along with his brothers and sisters; some of them never left, and to my dad, Honeywell was home. He told us many tales whilst we were growing up about his childhood and the antics he got up to. As he is no longer with us, it has been really nice to meet people whom he knew and shared his childhood with. Hearing them recall their experiences has helped me relive some of his tales.

After an appeal for interest was placed in the Barnsley Chronicle, we were inundated with people who wanted to be involved, whereby the Honeywell Reminiscences Group was created.

It is heartwarming to see people renew old friendships and listen to them talk. Whilst each has their own precious memories, it has not been an easy task to get people writing; many have not written anything for years, so for them a story would be out of the question, but they have written and I hope you will agree, when you read the book, their efforts have been worthwhile. It has convinced me 'we all have a story to tell.'

To our members we say a special thank you, without them this book could have not happened. Thank you for your time, it can never be replaced and for all the photographs and stories that have been contributed. Whilst it has not been possible to include all that we have collected, we hope the selection we have made helps the reader see quite clearly that the Honeywell area of Barnsley was a strong, caring and supportive community.

Why not indulge yourself in nostalgia; look to see if you are amongst the children featured in our school photographs, or maybe you were part of a celebration or even a work colleague. These could be your memories too.

With regard to the front cover photograph and the title 'The Happiest Street in Barnsley,' we have been told that Honeywell Street did indeed earn itself this title, a number of people have verified it. Folk remember the photographs being taken but not who took them or how the title came about. Some think the Barnsley Chronicle were involved, but we can't find any trace in the Barnsley Archives. Others think it was a Yorkshire Television competition, but although we have tried, we can't confirm this, so we prefer to 'just believe it,' and besides, what does it matter? To us, it reflects what our book is all about, which is a community.

However, we would like to say this book is not just about 'the Street,' but the whole area, and we believe it is a fitting tribute to the Honeywell Community.

We wanted to record these memories for future generations. Without it, how would they know anything about us? Times are changing so quickly; in this age of 'high tech,' children don't know about *'whips and tops,'* *'kick can'* or *'bunny wooding'* and much more. Coal mining is a thing of the past and so are most of the basic day-to-day tasks that needed to be done.

Hopefully, this book will give our descendants some idea of how we used to live, the times we lived through and what made us laugh and cry; it might even encourage others to record their own memories before it's too late.

Gloria Hesford (nee Phillips)

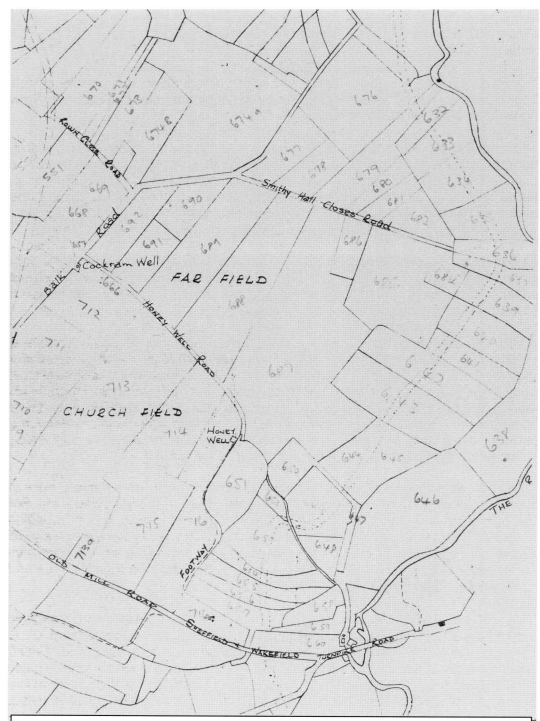

Ordnance Survey Map of 1777 of the Honeywell area – reproduced by **kind permission of Barnsley MBC's Archives and Local Studies Dept.**

FROM HONEY WELL TO HONEYWELL
Julie Johnson

Two main topics of conversation have arisen surrounding the making of this book. Firstly, where does the name Honeywell originate from, and secondly, how do we define the area.

Thinking about the name can conjure up images of the countryside, and warm, carefree sunny days, and as suggested by others on hearing the name – it sounds like a lovely place. Looking on the Ordnance Survey Map of the area, dated 1777 (courtesy of Barnsley Archives), the name Honey Well appears at the bottom of Honey Well Road (now known as Honeywell Lane).

Before the supply of piped water came into everyday use in households, nearly all communities and individuals were dependent upon wells and springs for their water. Wells, by definition, are man-made circular structures created to extract water from below ground; springs are a natural feature, where water wells up from underground rocks.

As Rob Wilson stated in his book, 'Holy Wells and Spas of South Yorkshire' (1991), *The area called Honeywell takes its name from Honey Well, whose water was regarded as being the sweetest in Barnsley.* This confirms what many local people have thought. In more recent times, as mentioned by Ronnie Smith, in his story 'The Smiths from Honeywell,' he states that *From Well View to dad's allotment ran a stream of pure spring water. This spring water was analysed and tested at Barnsley Town Hall, and was indeed found to be pure drinking water, which even during the hottest of summers stayed icy cold.*

Over the last sixty years or so, Honeywell has become a more defined area of Barnsley, although everyone has their own idea of where it begins and ends. For the purposes of this book, we have included what some may call surrounding areas. With this in mind, and using the Honeywell Community Centre, Honeywell Street, as a central point of reference, we have included: to the west, Cockerham Lane/Bridge Street; to the north, Willow Bank; to the east, the River Dearne and to the south, Eldon Street/Harborough Hill Road.

This area was originally dominated by fields, allotments and wasteland, alongside industries such as bleaching works, mining (coal and stone), paper making, glass making, nail works and transportation of goods via the Aire and Calder Navigation (Barnsley Canal). There were two pits in the immediate area: Honey Well Colliery (read Eric Phillips' story in this book), and the Old Stone Pit, where Stone Street now resides. Nowadays the area is largely made up of housing, after programmes of regeneration and modernisation have taken place. Honeywell has a rich diverse history, and the stories in this book reflect the lives of those living, going to school and working in Honeywell and the surrounding area.

We hope you enjoy reading these stories, and looking at the photographs and sketches we have included in this book. Do you have a connection with Honeywell? - Let us know.

Artist 'Andy Phillips' impression of days gone by

DOGS, PIGS AND DUCKS
Val Brown

My granddad came over from Huddersfield and met my gran who lived in Old Mill Lane. She became Sarah Elizabeth Elsworth and after they married at St Mary's Church in 1907, they moved to No. 34 Honeywell Street and all their six kids married from there. I was to visit this street regularly from about 1946 but always called my gran Metcalf, due to the fact that she had remarried after my granddad had died in1921. I still thought of her as Metcalf until I did my family tree and I realised it was not my paternal side's name.

Sarah Elizabeth Elsworth

I'm now a gran myself but often look back on the times I visited my gran's and wonder what my kids would think if I told them I had a DUCK which was loved to bits, but had a psychological problem due to thinking itself a guard dog!

To get to the back of No. 34 you had to go down a ginnel, which was a bad move as there was a guard duck lying in wait. You ventured down the ginnel at your own peril for the guard duck was waiting to pounce on any unsuspecting person. Raised up on its two legs, wings flapping and squealing, the visitor would be abused and chased back out, until the voice of its master was heard to shout it - then it was safe for you to continue and the guard went back to being a placid, loving duck.

I often wonder if there is anybody still living down there that remembers this family. When on my way to Asda I still take a sneaky look on Honeywell. My gran lived there until she became ill and moved to live with her daughter at Athersley which is where she died.

I have another great laugh for you, a story about a pig called Bessie. The story was handed down to my cousin by his mum, one of my gran's daughters, who married and lived in the same area. This pig was as useful as the duck; it was the leader of the blind (drunk). My cousin's dad used to go on the *pop*, get blind drunk and the pig would wait for him and take him home on its back.

Then there was the cockerel story. Meant for a Christmas dinner, the cockerels were pinched, had their necks wrung, put in a sack and carried home - only to jump out of the sack on to the table at twelve thirty calling: "cock a doodle doo" with two drunk men chasing them round the house.

There was also Liberace the mouse. My cousin's father and the man next door at No.12 Days Croft, went for a few beers, came home with a very nice stagger on and decided to finish the night at No.12. Bottles in their hands they sat on the sofa, very comfy with their backs to the piano and started to sing a little. Suddenly there was music! A little out of tune with their singing, but on hearing the music both men *paled*, flung their bottles and tipped the sofa over in a panic! It soon came to their attention that a mouse had decided to join the fun and take a piano lesson. Both men rolled with laughing and left the mouse to get on with his lesson.

Large families, large stories!

MEMORIES OF HONEYWELL MANY YEARS AGO
Annie Storey(nee Barrett)

Is it my imagination, or were the summers so much sunnier and the winters so much crisper and brighter in my childhood? When I think of Honeywell, I dream of cheerful times spent with my cousin Maureen, when we wandered by the side of the allotments opposite, where Granddad and Grandma Phillips had brought up their large brood of children at number 112 Honeywell Street. We would follow the path down to the fields where the canal quietly wound its way.

Our Maureen and I never knew grandma; she died aged 50 before we were born and we only have one photo of her. My mother said that she had long black hair and brown eyes.
I can remember my granddad. He had a kindly, sensitive face and was a smallish man with a wiry frame. He wore a moustache, as most men did in those days. He met grandmother, Annie Hall, when she lived down Smithies Lane and he lived at a house in Honeywell Fields.

They married on Christmas Day 1905 at St Mary's Church, becoming Mr. and Mrs. Phillips, residing at 112 Honeywell Street. Granddad always wore his flat cap; my mother said he would never be parted from it, as she thought he was sensitive about having a bald head. He was so sensitive that he was a vegetarian, rather unusual for a miner in those days; he couldn't bear to eat any part of what had been a living creature. Unfortunately, this proved to be his downfall; mother said that he developed pernicious anaemia. A week before he died, my mother said that he was persuaded to eat a tiny piece of liver, but it was too late and his weakened body gave up. Mother also said that he had never got over the death of his wife, and had died of a broken heart.

They reared a large family. The boys were: my Uncle Andrew, Uncle George, Uncle Tommy, and Uncle Bill, the youngest one. The girls were Auntie Lena, Frances (my mother), Auntie Olive, and Auntie Mary, (my cousin Maureen's mother). There was another child, Gladys, who died at three of, I think, pneumonia. My mother said that Gladys was a most beautiful child with a halo of golden curls.

Mother always said that though they were a large brood, they loved each other and they could run to their father any time with problems. Besides being a miner, he worked on Saturdays sweeping Barnsley market up after the traders had gone home. One day, in the rubbish, he saw something glittering. It was a gold ring in a pretty design, set with diamonds. He took it home and gave it to Annie, his wife, who was thrilled with it and wore it till her death. Upon her passing, my mother gave up her job at the Paper Mill, deferred her wedding to my father for five years, and stayed at home to look after her father and brothers. As a reward, grandfather gave her the ring.

It eventually passed to me and I gave it to my eldest daughter Debra, who had greatly admired it for many years. I expect that it will pass to Paige my granddaughter in time. She has recently given birth to our second great grandson Oscar; her first son is named Oakley. They are a delightful little family and I expect that if she ever has a little girl, the ring will pass on indefinitely and they will know the story of its origin.

I once asked my mother what kind of sleeping arrangements they had for such a large family in a small house. She answered that the girls slept in their parents' bedroom and the boys slept in the other. They slept top-to-toe as well, like the proverbial sardines; it must have been very uncomfortable in hot weather.

My cousin Maureen and I have always thought of ourselves as sisters because we are so close. We were chatting about this book and she narrated a little story to me about something that happened to her as a child at Honeywell. It could be viewed as humorous, but not to her, poor thing.

Alongside the steps leading to the allotments, as previously mentioned, were some earth closets; we knew them as middens. Maureen said that when she was five she fell into one. Aunt Mary dragged her to the bottom house in Honeywell Street where they had been doing the washing, and dumped her in the tub to rub her clean. What a horrible experience. I expect it may have been on a Monday, because if the weather was fine and dry, it was traditional to wash at the beginning of the week, iron in the middle, and clean the house on Thursday and Friday. I remember we kids running up the back yards, in between the clothes props, banging our mucky hands on clean sheets as they flapped in the wind. There must have been many a swear word at the end of the day from

Barrett Family

the ladies who had toiled so lugubriously with just a tub, a scrubbing board, and a *posser* or a peggy stick - no washing machine for them.

This reminds me of another incident Maureen was involved in with me. I wouldn't say that James Street is Honeywell, but I think it's a close extension, being on the other side of Eldon Street where another two cousins of mine lived.

When Maureen and I were around eight to ten years old, the same age as our cousin Ken, Auntie Olive, his mother, used to invite Maureen and myself to tea on Sundays after we'd finished playing at Honeywell. Auntie Olive always had a proper linen tablecloth on the table and some nice crockery, even for us children. Unfortunately, we let ourselves down by constantly misbehaving, mainly laughing and giggling. Auntie Olive got increasingly irritated, but this went on throughout the meal.

One day, I came home from school and found my mother standing there with arms folded. She said, "I've had our Olive onto me, and our Mary, over the way you kids behave at the tea table; she says that you laugh at her." I protested, "It's not at Auntie Olive, Mam, we like her, we just look at each other and can't stop laughing, especially when our Ken puts his hand to his mouth." Mother persisted, "But what do you find to laugh at?" "Nothing." I replied weakly. Mother retorted, "They take 'em away for less than that. They'll be coming in white coats and carting you all away."

The vision of our Maureen, Ken and me being spirited away by men in white coats convulsed me. My mother spoke again, "See, you're at it again, I'm ashamed of you! First you laugh at our Olive, and now at me. Do you know what's wrong with you?" I shook my head between explosive bursts of mirth. Mother walked away, then came back and stuck her face close to mine. "You're ignorant! Just plain ignorant!" And she stalked away.

I did learn a lesson in tolerance and understanding that day. With regard to some of my own grandchildren many years later, I recognise their behaviour in my own. I believe that children around the world like to take a rise out of adults, but I think of the time when I was young. I too was very full of youthful misdemeanours.

I think there were similarities between Kingstone where I was born and Honeywell. They both had long streets of old terrace houses surrounded by woods, fields and long walk areas. The canal at Honeywell had its own bridges, the Thirty-Two Steps being one of them. This has not existed for many years now, but I remember diligently counting the steps as I climbed up them and down the other side. By comparison, the ABC steps in Locke Park were of interest too.

Another similarity between Kingstone and Honeywell was that we had a grandparent in each area. Granddad Phillips in Honeywell, and Grandma Barrett in Kingstone, the former, serious and studious, and the latter, lively, who would sometimes throw caution to the wind, but nevertheless, had a warm loving heart. All in all, I think I was a fortunate child to have two such choices.

MY UNCLE TOMMY
Annie Storey

Poor old Uncle Tommy, Yorkshire born and bred,
Always getting into scrapes, or so his kinfolk said,
My mother told me a tale or two
One involving toe-rag stew.
Their mother was preparing dinner,
When up popped Tommy, the little sinner.
He whirled a sock around and round,
Landing in meat, three half-pence a pound.
It simmered for hours, made the meat tasty.
When grandma found it, she thought,
"Can't be hasty,
I've got a great big family to feed,
It's not as if they really need,
To know the sock is in the stew,
I'll dole this out, and then come true."
They ate their fill,
"My that tastes good,"
Grandma said, "Did you find any mud?
Tommy's sock's in for you to savour,
I hope it didn't alter the flavour,
I'll catch the little sod, and tan his hide,
Cos in my dinners I take some pride.
He's a little rascal, that's for sure,
But if you liked it, you can have some more."
My mother saw the twinkle in Gran's eye,
Knowing she couldn't swat a fly.
She knew that she would never bellow,
Cos Uncle Tommy was a loveable fellow.

Thomas Phillips Snr, Tommy & George Phillips, Honeywell Street.

ILLNESS AND HARD WORK
Sid Williams

As a kid my home was 18 Honeywell Street. It was a three-bedroom house and my mother and dad had seven kids, Hilda, Eileen, Pamela, Albert, Billy, Sidney and David - so it didn't take long to *brod* a peg rug with all those hands!

I had a garden on Honeywell where I used to keep pigs, hens and geese. I would fatten two pigs for Christmas, one to market and one to cut up down the cellar where we had a big stone slab like a table. Yes you could eat your dinner off the floor in my mother's cellar.

I went to Eldon Street School. There was no gym, we used to pull big doormats into the playground, but after all that, when the teacher came out he made me sit on the step as I had a leaking valve in my heart and I wasn't allowed to exert myself. I also got my boots for nothing because I had a poorly father.

Elsie Williams

For entertainment I remember going to The Electric Theatre on Eastgate or *Lec*, as we knew it, on Saturday mornings. It cost one or two pennies and I saw cowboy pictures like Buck Jones and Hopalong Cassidy.

I also remember sledging down Harborough Hills Road, ending up at the Tollgate Pub, but there were no cars and lorries like there are today - besides, the hill was like glass - fantastic!

I started work when I was fourteen years old at the Ceag bulb company in Queen's Road. I was a carrier, fetching steel from the stores to make miner's lamps. I stayed there five years then I went to Redfearns in the fitting shop where I worked for forty odd years. My granddad, dad and three of my brothers, Albert, Billy and David also worked there and my dad's brother Jabus was the chief engineer.

My sister Eileen worked at the Star Paper Mill during the war, sorting salvage paper, so we used to get some free comics.

As I mentioned earlier I had a problem with my heart and had rheumatic fever when I was nine or ten years old so they didn't want me in the army because of my leaking heart valve.

Later I got a tumour on my kidney which I had removed in 1989 when I was fifty-nine years old. In March 1989 I got pleurisy, then shingles. Redundancy was on offer at Redfearns in 1990 and I have not worked since, but I am still here!

'Sid Williams' with friends in Blackpool

GRANDMA AND GRANDDAD WATERSON
Mary Lipscombe

My mother was the third of four sisters, born to John and Annie Waterson. The following are not my memories, but are authentic and accurate.

My grandma was born Annie Hebden on 16 November 1891, in Spa Cottage, Eldon Street North, Barnsley. She came from a big family, as was the norm in those days; her parents were John William and Sarah Hebden (nee Conduit). Upon leaving school, Annie went to work at Taylor's weaving mill, Peel Street, Barnsley. (As a point of interest Barnsley linen was famous, the industry being as important as coal mining, in this area).

When Annie was about eighteen years old, she met my granddad, John (Jack) Waterson, who was born on 18th June 1889. Annie and Jack were married in February 1912 and lived at 74 Old Mill Lane, Barnsley. Sarah Ellen (Sarah) their first daughter soon made an appearance followed by Annie, exactly two years later, then by my mother, Norah, exactly two years after Annie. Mary Alice (Mary) the youngest daughter was born when my mother was two years and four months old. Jack continued working in the pit until he went into the army when The Great War started (World War 1).

Annie Waterson

He served in France and I still have many silk embroidered cards, which he sent regularly to my grandma and his little girls. The messages written on the back of these cards are very touching to read, they are so full of love and affection for his family. (My mother once wryly remarked that he must have had at least two home leaves from

23

France, leaving my mother and Auntie Mary on the way, after each leave).

In October 1918 just before the end of the war he narrowly escaped death when he was wounded. After his discharge from the army he returned to work in the pit, then in August 1919 he went to work at Newera concrete works, Smithies, Barnsley. My grandma had been anxious that he did not return to work in the coal mine; she thought that it was too dangerous. I must say that my granddad was a very handsome young man, who was liked by everyone who knew him; all he lived for was his wife and little girls. The three eldest were allowed to go and stand at the end of Honeywell Street to wait for him coming home from work. One of my aunts recalls shouting Dadda as he approached and he would scoop up all three of them together, giving them a hug.

In Barnsley it was the tradition to hold the October Fair Day on Churchfields. This was apparently the only holiday which families had. In 1919 the fair was held on 11 October. The following is in quotes and was told to me by my grandma:

"On October Fair Day, your granddad, got up for work; he would not take a day off because we couldn't afford it. I can remember him giving all of us a kiss before he set off; within a minute he was back. I asked him what was wrong and he said nothing, he just felt uneasy. This happened three times; I told him to take the day off work because he must be feeling tired, but he refused. I saw him pass the window; it was quite early in the morning, and I was busy getting the four children ready to take them to the fair. Your granddad had been gone for quite some time when I heard the ambulance going past our front door. I went cold and I thought 'it is Jack.' I asked my neighbour to come in to keep an eye on the children, grabbed a shawl and went running down Old Mill Lane.

I reached the concrete works, just in time to see Jack being put into the ambulance on a stretcher; he looked as if he was asleep. There was quite a crowd of people gathered around and I heard someone say that one man was dead. I ran back home and by this time my mother had come to our house, which was a rare event although she only lived round the corner in John Edward Street. She had objected to your granddad being a Roman Catholic and the fact that our children had been baptised in the Roman Catholic Church.

She told me to stay with the children, whilst she went up to Beckett Hospital to see what was happening. I was too numb to do anything, except sit rocking your auntie Mary, who was only ten months old. I can't even remember now which neighbour took your mam, our Sarah and Annie to be looked after. I sat in the chair for ages and kept saying 'Please God, don't let Jack be dead, whatever state he is in I will look after him.' When it got to the afternoon I couldn't stand it any longer, so I set off with your auntie Mary to go to the hospital. I met my mother coming down Old Mill Lane and from the look on her face I knew that your granddad had died. He had been killed instantly and his work mate, Arthur McCoubrey had died in hospital from a fractured skull. The only mark on your granddad was a bruise on his mouth. The coroner could not find evidence of the cause of his death, other than a concrete column had collapsed on the two men, breaking your granddad's neck."

I could give more details, but I will finish by telling you that it took quite some time for things to be sorted out. My grandma had no money, and with four children, aged seven, five, three and ten months old, she had no option but to swallow her pride and they lived on donations from the poor box of Saint Mary's Church. Eventually she received £200 compensation and when she had spent that, she went back to her old job as a weaver, while her mother reluctantly cared for the children. She moved to the linen mill at Redbrook which was owned by Hickson Lloyd & King, working there until she was sixty years old.

Honeywell featured very much in my childhood. My grandma Annie Hebden lived in John Edward Street with her Mum and Dad and her sisters Ada (known as Dolly) the eldest; then came Annie (grandma), Alice, Mary (known as Polly), Elizabeth (known as Tiddy) and Eva; there were also two brothers, John and Richard.

Unfortunately I know very little about grandma's family, other than her father was called Richard and her mother was called Sarah, who was born in Manchester. How she came to live in Barnsley I don't know. Maybe it was when she married Richard.

I can remember Great Grandma Hebden who lived with her daughter Dolly. She died in 1946. My mother used to take me to see her and I was always scared stiff. I can never remember seeing her out of bed. She had very long white hair which draped over her shoulders. She always reminded me of a witch; this may seem disrespectful but that was how I felt. Her husband Richard had died some years before and whilst at the graveside at his funeral, his son, Richard (known as Dick) said, "I shall never get over this." He was nineteen years old. Within three weeks, the family were standing at Dick's graveside. The poor lad had had a carbuncle on the back of his neck, blood poisoning set in and it killed him.

John (Jack) Waterson

The Hebden family had a very hard life along with everybody else in those days. As I said earlier Grandma went to work at the age of thirteen at Taylor's linen mill.

I particularly remember Auntie Dolly who was one of the kindest people I knew. She hardly ever went out because she was so ashamed of her size. It was wonderful to be cuddled by her; she was so soft and welcoming and my main memory of her is that she was always baking.

FOND MEMORIES OF HONEYWELL
Irene Bostwick

The following is an account of my earliest memories of living in Honeywell.

I was born Irene Graham on 20th August 1913 in Albion Terrace, Barnsley. My family moved to Honeywell Street when I was a baby. I had a sister called Jessie who was two years older, a younger sister Jean, two younger brothers called Donald and James and my mum and dad who were called Hannah and Peter. James was born in 1919 and was a poorly baby with diphtheria. He spent some time in Kendray Hospital and we were very worried about him.

The row of fourteen terraced houses where I lived was on the same side as, and next to, the shop currently known as Dot's shop. The first one was my home, number 27. Our neighbours in the row were called Barton, Hunt, Garnett, Taylor, Ellis, Pearson, Kenworthy, England, Nutton, Parkin, Farrell, Bailey and Broadhead.

Sanitation for the houses consisted of two adjoining water toilets, for every two properties, and a bin store housing four bins, for four properties. In the middle of the row at the rear, there was a path leading to our gardens, where we would play shop with bits of pot and glass. Tin baths were used on bath nights and ours was stored indoors, although some families kept theirs hung outside. Mother would stand on the step and call our names if we were wanted, to make sure we weren't far away. The terraced houses on the opposite side to number 27 and further along Honeywell Street had gardens at the front.

Looking down from the back of the house you could see Monk Bretton Priory and the canal. You could also hear the paper mill buzzer at 12 o'clock, which was very loud. Redfearn's factory was on Twibell Street, and a nail factory was down by Canal Street. The Old Mill Tannery was down North Eldon Street near the gasometer. The men who raced pigeons passed through our back yard, down to the gardens and on to John Edward Street, where there was a ginnel through to the Keel fields near the Keel Inn.

During WW1 my father was in the Yorkshire/Lancashire Regiment, a Barnsley Pal who received the Military Medal. His brothers Jim, Alec and two others were also in the war and one, Oliver, who was only nineteen years of age, got killed in action. Mr. Crawley, who lived down Old Mill Lane, was a policeman known as Bobby Jim. He used to knock on the windows of the houses to get people to pull their blackouts down. I was taken to Meadow Street by my mum, along with my sister and another lady when the air raids sounded. The Zeppelins used to come overhead. I remember it being a frightening time. Bobby Jim's son used to play the bugle in the Salvation Army band. A relation of his still lives in that house, her name is Rita Crawley.

After the war, when I was five, I went to Beckett Street Infants School. While I was there I learned arithmetic, composition (English) and times tables - basically the three Rs - reading, writing and arithmetic which stood you in good stead throughout your life. At play times we played ball games, hop scotch and bats and shuttle cocks if you were well off. You would throw the ball against the wall, clap, twist and fold between throws – this was one of my favourite games, or we would just chat in groups with friends. Mothers used to play skipping with the children. The school regime was quite strict and we went home at lunchtimes.

Aged eight, I went to Eldon Street School, which was an all-girls school. The separate boys' school was next door. Many of the boys were good footballers. There was a tuck shop across the road from the school. I remember wearing boots at the time that were very heavy, and I hated them.

Different men would come round selling their wares. A man at the bottom of the steps would have a basket and shout: "white bread, brown bread, tea-cakes, sally lunns, and scones." There was also a man selling huge blocks of salt from a cart; a fish cart selling fish and rabbit and Mr. Cowdell selling Hokey Pokey, which was like blocks of ice cream. A man repaired wooden tubs and men sharpened knives. The rag and bone man shouted: "rags, bones and rabbit skins!" If people took him rags or other items, he would give them something in exchange, like a goldfish or a windmill on a stick.

Dixon was the local coal merchant; you could take a wheelbarrow and buy coal from him a couple of houses away from the Honeywell Pub. Mrs. Bedford had the shop on the bottom corner of Honeywell Lane (1920's). Milk was normally tinned, but you could get fresh from a friend, Barbara Jones. Teal's shop a couple of doors away from the pub sold everything and opened until late. There was a shop down Eldon Street/New Bridge Street called Thorpe's where you could get savoury ducks; inside there was a big tray of them and a jug of gravy. You could eat it as a meal and people would come from far and near to get them. It was a pork butcher, so they must have been made up of pork with herbs and spices.

At Earnshaw's, another shop across the road, they used to have big glass jars of pickled onions and piccalilli and you could take a container and buy a small amount, as it was sold loose. At the top of John Edward Street there was a shop first called Nunn's, then Severn's and Gunhouses. I used to run errands and go into town for my mother. We walked everywhere.

Dot's shop then, was named Bates' and later Rivers'. The shop consisted of two houses fronting Old Mill Lane. The first one sold pianos and the lower one tuned them. Behind the counter was a shelf which had big glass containers. In them there would be many medications and you could take a container or a glass and they would measure out an ounce of Indian Brandy, an ounce of Syrup of Squills (probably for bronchitis), an ounce of cut moss for baby's gums, glycerine and things like that. You could buy a little twist of Beachams Pills or Bile Beans.

I remember having whooping cough and my mother took me to where they were mending roads with tar, as the smell was a good remedy for it. Dr Eskages was a pit doctor who held his surgery in a house down Old Mill Lane. Girls would go in for medicine. His remedies were so good that his cough stuff was known by his name; "You want a dose of Dr Eskages?" He was a friendly doctor and would help if you were poorly. Neighbours were very friendly and especially helpful if you needed goose grease for your chest.

Mrs Smith had a fish shop on Sheffield Road and also cut hair. I remember having to have mine cut short. It cost thru' pence and I didn't like it, but money was scarce in those days. After the war my father, Peter, played football for Darfield when they won the Beckett Hospital Cup. At this time he worked on the pit top at Grimethorpe. Sometimes you could hear a pit buzzer which meant that someone had been killed in the pit, therefore men didn't have to go to work the next day.

When there was a funeral, children used to gather around the house door and two big black horses with big black tales and plumes used to draw the carriage carrying the coffin. A lady would bring cake and biscuits for the horses and give the children some as well. Sometimes there would be artificial flowers in a glass globe placed on the grave.

I took the Eleven Plus exam before leaving Eldon Street Junior School. Some who passed went to the Girls High School on Huddersfield Road, and others who passed like me, could go to Mark Street School, which was opposite Holyrood Church in the town centre. The Longcar Central School came in during that time and you could go there without passing your Eleven Plus. Before starting senior school I had a lengthy stay in hospital and it was some twelve months later when I actually attended Grove Street School.

Grove Street School at that time catered for those who liked and were gifted in

Irene can be seen in this picture on the front row – far right-hand side

performing arts such as poetry reading, performing and music. Miss Elsie Chambers used to coach students in elocution and deportment and was a perfectionist. I joined the Junior Choral Society, and Miss Chambers put me forward for a Gilbert & Sullivan operetta called 'Princess Zara' where I played Queen Butterfly. Miss Chambers produced it and the conductor was a Mr. Whealdon. The operetta took place at the Public Hall (now known as the Civic Hall) and I was about thirteen or fourteen at the time. I could see my name on the production advertisement on the display board outside, when I was passing by with my mum. I enjoyed reciting poetry and practiced in the school hall.

I was entered in the Barnsley Music Festival at the Public Hall along with thirty-eight other children, and won first place, receiving ninety-six marks. Mr. Davies, director of education at the time, was adjudicator. I won the second year too. A photograph appeared in the Barnsley Chronicle in 1925, when I was in standard six, advertising our achievements.

As a little girl I once went on a day trip to Cleethorpes in a charabanc. The trip was organised by someone who worked at CEAG. We took our own sandwiches to eat there, but didn't see the sea, as it rained all day. On a Saturday afternoon you could go to the pictures called the *Penny Rush* and I took my brother. It cost a penny each – hence the name. This was at the Electric Theatre down Eastgate. Films of the day were 'Dr Fu Manchu' which was a serial and I loved it. Also 'Fashion for the Fair Sex.' Betty Balfour is a screen name I remember.

Sometimes Mum used to take my youngest sister Jean to see a play featuring the Denville Players at the Theatre Royal. I was affectionately nicknamed 'Trotters' when mum was in a good mood. When I was going to see a pantomime, I was told by mum that if I sat still until 5.30 p.m. she would take me to see 'Babes in the Wood.' I was bursting with excitement, and couldn't wait to go, which made the task of sitting still all the more difficult! I remember the song 'Give Me a Cosy Little Corner in an Armchair for Two' from this. Another time I went to see 'Mother Goose.' I went up the steps to the gallery where I stood in front of the barrier. A song from this I remember was 'Around Her Neck She Wore a Yellow Ribbon.'

I attended Regent Street chapel, where I again got involved in poetry reading. I won a place in poetry reading for the Eisteddfod for the Sunday schools. We also attended Brownies at the chapel and had concerts. Regent Street was a lovely chapel with a very tall spire. There was also a small chapel on Bridge Street with a ginnel nearby which led onto Honeywell Street at the side of the Honeywell pub.

I used to walk with other chapel people on the Whitsuntide Walk. We used to practice hymns, and on the day would walk behind our banner to Market Hill. Everyone stood and sang there, and Mr. Frudd would mark time as the conductor. After singing, we all walked around the streets in the town centre. Every year a different route would be taken. Afterwards, we went back to Sunday school for tea, which consisted of potted meat sandwiches and a drink of tea -

they never tasted so good! Then off to a field in Honeywell Lane to play sports, mostly running for prizes. The next day there would be a trip to Cumberworth on the train for the day. The minister at Regent Street chapel was a Mr. Taylor who lived at the Manse at 6 Huddersfield Road, which is currently the doctor's surgery.

I remember one Christmas. It was at the morning service, when Mr Taylor, who had just finished his address to the children, came down from the pulpit to shake our hands and wish us all a merry Christmas. When he came to me he said: "This is from Santa Claus of the church." He waved his hand around the congregation and gave me a £1 note. I was amazed and smiled at him, thanked everyone and flew down Regent Street to give it to my mother with great joy. It was as if Jesus gave it to me. I think it was a prosperous congregation.

In 1926 the General Strike took place and when a bell rang at St Barnabas Church, children could go to a tin structure there and get a free meal. I don't know who paid for the food or how long it lasted, but local volunteers ran it.

One day I was standing outside our house when a girl I knew asked me if I was coming to sell flags. The door was ajar, and I shouted, "Can I sell flags?" The answer was, "Don't go away," but I went. We went to the Cooper Art Gallery on Church Street. We stood at the top of Old Mill Lane with the box of flags and a collecting box. The sun was shining and ladies passed by with lovely hats, perfume and baskets for their shopping. They would buy a flag and I would pin it on them - so pleased with myself! One lady looked in her purse and only had a half-penny in change. I said, "It's quite alright you can put anything in." So she put the half-penny in the box. I was so pleased and happy. I looked along Church Street and saw my dad stepping out. I hurriedly gave the box to the girl and shouted, "My dad! My dad!" I flew down Old Mill Lane. The girl asked him, "Is she coming out to play?" My dad told her, "No, she's going upstairs." I was in disgrace.

A long time after the incident a letter came to our house. My mother read it to me. It was a letter thanking me for collecting so much money. I stood in amazement as I had enjoyed it. Mother said, "You were in trouble over that weren't you?" "Yes," I said, and she told me to go to school.

Miss Chambers was always putting on plays and I remember once playing the White Rabbit in 'Alice in Wonderland.' Annie Ellis was Alice, and we used to practice in the toilets. The art mistress was Miss Dora Hague and her father, Edwin Hague, was the principal of the Art School which was on the top floor of the Public Hall. Alice and White Rabbit (Annie and I) were chosen to pose as subjects for the art students to draw for the day. We had to stand still, in a pose, within a chalked circle and not move, except for a break at lunchtime. We were rewarded for our efforts with a 1 lb box of chocolates and five shillings.

I left Grove Street school aged 14 to look after my younger brother Donald, who was 13 years younger than me. Most girls from Honeywell, on leaving school worked at the shirt factory in Stocks Lane or at the CEAG factory where they made light bulbs. My sister Jean worked there in the office. Men tended to work at Redfearns or the paper mill. I was still a teenager when I left Honeywell.

Since Irene gave us her 'Fond Memories of Honeywell' story, she has sadly passed away. Her son John, has kindly agreed that we can include her story in this book.

UNCLE JACK
Don Booker MBE

My interest in four-wheeled travel stems from the interest shown in me as a lad by my Uncle Jack (Booker).

When summer came around he would say, "Get thi sen four wheels an I'll make thi a trolley." Off I would go around Old Bridge Street, to find a family with a pram that was near the end of its usefulness.

They were usually parked beneath front windows of a long row of stone - fronted terraced houses. I would knock and ask the woman if she wanted to sell her pram. Times were hard in the 1930's and more often than not I would come away with the complete child's pram after paying two shillings and sixpence (12½ p now).

Uncle Jack Booker

If I could manage to negotiate for a high, coach-built pram like a Silver Cross, I would be really pleased, as they had two large wheels and two small wheels, and I knew from experience that the trolley would have good steering and road holding.

I always looked forward to the summer, not for a trip to Blackpool but for a trolley. 'Mi Uncle Jack' was an expert, a self-taught joiner who had the task of repairing wooden coal wagons in the open, usually in a siding off Old Mill Lane.

He had a stable-type workshop in the backyard of his house. In the corner, standing on bricks, was an old wardrobe in which he stored his tools.

I would strip down the pram and hand the axles and wheels to Uncle Jack, who would build the trolley from spare wood. A steel bolt held together the front steering board and the main part of the trolley. We found that the steel ceiling roses that held those fancy light bowls which hung on chains, made ideal steering linkages!

Andy Phillips

If wood was short, I would go to Eldon Street North Co-op and buy for sixpence, a Gamages soapbox which gave the trolley an instant body with appalling aerodynamics.

To me, a trolley and the mobility were exciting because I had never had a pedal car or a three-wheeled bike.

I spent hours with 'mi Uncle Jack' in that shed. He smoked Woodbines and threw his tabs on the brick floor. When he turned away, I picked them up and dashed down the yard to the closet where I finished them off.

It appeared I was on a good thing until one day my dad asked: "What's this I hear about you smoking lad?" I was shocked and said I didn't know what he was talking about.
"Yer Uncle Jack sez he's seen yer picking up off floor," he replied. He told me to stop it – and I haven't smoked since. From the corner of his eye 'mi Uncle Jack' had seen me up to my tricks.

At that time, most youngsters dreaded the Eleven Plus examination. Most were promised a new bike if they passed it – what a dream. But I had no chance. Three years later the offer was made to me - if I could pass the entrance examination to Barnsley Junior Technical School. At the same time I sat a special examination for a teacher's course at Longcar Central School. I passed them both for I had developed a lot at Raley School.

Before that I had attended Burton Road School, where I think I spent more time cleaning out the fish pond than studying the *three R's*.

Although I was successful in the two exams, the promise of the new bike had been made, but never materialised because in my dad's trade – he was a fell monger, dealing with sheep's pelts and grading wool – things were bad in the summer, and there were weeks when he didn't work. For months I had looked with envy at cycle dealers showrooms, not at gleaming bikes – there was no chrome in wartime - but at matt black pedal cycles.

No, I didn't get that new bike. I was back in the workshop with 'mi Uncle Jack' who said I could have his bike which had been re-built but was rusty. The bike with no name was re-built again but spares were in short supply. I used sticky tape to repair punctures, and often had three a day because the inner tubes would nip against the wheel rim. That bike was upside-down resting on its handlebars and seats more than it was on its wheels.

Eventually, when things got better, I re-built it with a three-speed rear hub, a Lucas Dynamo System and chrome semi–sporting handlebars. It was kept in the coal-house but one morning I found it had been stolen. It was never replaced.

To this day, I still think about the bike I would have loved, such as an Elswick sports model. They say what you haven't had you'll never miss – but I miss the thrills I'm sure those bikes provided for a teenager.

HONEYWELL GROVE
Allan Williamson

I was born in 1937 and lived in the Honeywell area until 1971. In my opinion it was a childhood paradise living on Honeywell Grove.

Being an un-adopted road, it was more like a wide cart track, which was bone dry in the summer and had deep ruts of water in winter. As kids, when we were walking from school, we used to jump over one rut to the next to avoid the mud. This cart track went right through to Smithies Lane with various streets branching off, and much like Honeywell Grove, they too had unmade roads.

Issott Street and Aqueduct Street were only wide footpaths leading to allotments on either side, and the Dearne and Dove Canal ran along the bottom. From the edge of the allotments to the first privately owned semi detached house, where old Mr. Perkins lived, was a field known to us as Farmer Wright's field. From the last semi detached house there was a cart track that ran at the back of the gardens to Farmer Wright's stone built house. This house stood at the edge of the field and was behind old Mr. Perkins garden. I can vaguely remember Farmer Wright walking down the track, to his house, shotgun over his shoulder and a brace of ducks dangling from the gun. I don't know what happened to him, but the house became empty and derelict and was finally demolished.

HONEYWELL GROVE
Katherine Symcox

Until the 1960's there were just five terraced houses and fourteen blocks of semi detached houses built by Hibberts of Honeywell. No proper road was laid, so in winter the un-adopted road became rutted and very muddy.

Also at this time, a big building programme of council houses and flats started, and to make matters worse heavy lorries were used to bring in the materials required. People going out for the evening, to the pub or to a dance, had to walk from their homes in Wellington boots as far as Rockingham Street, before they could change into shoes. Once they had changed their shoes, they would then find a safe place under a bush to hide their Wellingtons until they picked them up later. It was once said that an ambulance collecting a pregnant woman refused to come down the street in case it got stuck.

WHEN WE FINALLY GOT A BUS
Sue Basford (nee Frost)

We finally got a bus in Honeywell during the sixties. It was quite exciting; people were stood at the bottom of the lane to watch the first one arrive. The housewives, who did most of the shopping, were very relieved as it was a long walk from town with heavy bags, especially in bad weather.

The bus drove from town and along Honeywell Street, to the end of Rockingham Street, turned round by the orphanage and drove back to town. We could never understand why you could catch it at the bottom of Honeywell Lane into town, but had to get off outside the Co-op when you came home. It was very useful when we went into town at night; my parents watched for the bus coming while we got ready, and by the time it had gone to turn round, we were at the bus stop to catch it.

Feast Week was when the pits shut down for two weeks and everyone went on their annual holidays. Most of the families went to Blackpool or Cleethorpes; when we arrived at the station it was very exciting to see the large steam train, and we tried to get a compartment where we could all sit together.

Early in the morning, the lads on Honeywell would be out with their wooden trolleys to carry your cases up to the station. Father would give them a tip, then off they would speed back to carry the next load. The trolleys were made out of bits of wood and pram wheels, with rope to pull or guide them. No one could afford taxis, and there was no bus to town, so you relied on the boys being theto carry your luggage.

THE SMITHS OF HONEYWELL
Ronnie Smith

The Smiths lived at 63 Honeywell Street. There was Dad (Jim), Mother (Ivy) sons Jim, Ronnie, Eric, Peter, Albert and daughter Muriel (Albert and Muriel were twins).

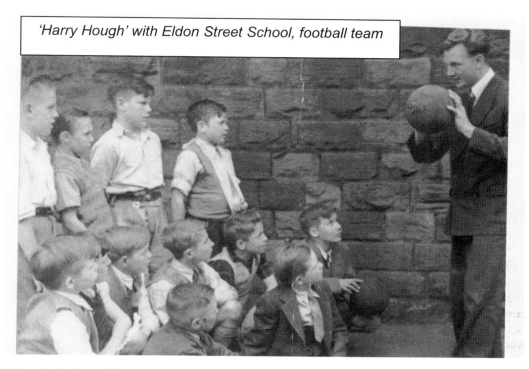

'Harry Hough' with Eldon Street School, football team

I (Ronnie) played football for Eldon Street School's all winning team in 1952 when they won the Football League Knockout Cup. That year the school's cricket team won the Cricket Shield, scoring one hundred and eight, throughout the season. I scored thirty-eight. The football team won every game it played, making Mr. Sheerian and Mr. Sykes very proud teachers. The home games were played on the Dearne Fields and the cup final against Agnes Road School was played at Redfearns' sports ground which was next to the canal. Over two thousand people turned up to watch the match that day; Eldon Street won, 3 – 0. The players that came from Honeywell were Doug Lovatt (goalkeeper), Peter Christon (right full back), Melvin Charlesworth (right wing), and I played inside left.

Mr. Harry Hemingway, our next-door neighbour, always gave me two shillings and sixpence if I scored a goal. When I went to Barnsley Central School, on Mark Street, I used to run home every afternoon at 4 'o'clock to watch sport on Mr. Hemingway's black and white television. In those days there were only two households that had televisions on Honeywell Street, the other person being Mr. Dick Carr.

Dad had two large allotments on Honeywell. He won a gold medal for his gardening skills and was known for miles around, particularly for his large blooms of chrysanthemums and all kinds of vegetables. *Honeywellers*, would order their vegetables for the weekend, and we would take them up from the allotments; cabbages, cauliflowers, forty to fifty pounds of kidney/runner beans, turnips carrots, beetroot etc.

From Well View to dad's allotment ran a stream of pure spring water. Dad routed it to run into a cast iron bath which he used for his garden. The overflow ran into a dyke and down to the canal by the side of the *Nail Oyle*. This spring water was analysed and tested at Barnsley Town Hall and was indeed found to be pure drinking water, which even during the hottest of summers stayed icy cold.

I used to go up Market Hill to the Market place, collecting pig snap for my dad's pigs. Then on Sunday afternoons, go on Mottram Street, James Street and Honeywell Street where people left out potato peelings, bread etc; for me to collect on my trolley onto which I tied a dustbin.

Dad always had a pig slaughtered for Christmas time, and Mr. Walt Gunhouse, who had the shop at the top of John Edward Street opposite the Honeywell Inn, always wanted the pig's head, to make potted meat.

Occupants of the Garden House (a cottage that was situated in the gardens) were Lily and Jack Armin. They owned the allotments and collected rent from the tenants; when they moved out Tommy and Doris Phillips, along with their five children, moved in. Less than two years later they too moved out. The cottage was demolished and the gardens were claimed on a compulsory order by Barnsley Council to be used for developing the houses you see today. However, it took years for them to get started and my dad was devastated. He had cultivated and looked after his garden for over fifty years.

Honeywell was a great place to grow up. As kids we played football, cricket and other games in the back yards, although Mr. Ward used to chase us out because we broke too many windows.

We played football in Dockertys field, where the flats are now, or on Willow Bank. Also as kids, we swam in the hot waters which came from the Star Paper Mill (where the Asda is now). Mischievous night (4 November) was a lot of fun for us kids, but not a lot for the older end, although mischief was all we got up to. We did things like the *Bull Roar*, putting newspaper up drain pipes and then lighting it, which caused the roaring noise. It used to sound quite loud from inside the house. Another trick we had was to stick a drawing pin into the window frame, fasten a piece of string or catgut to it, and tie a knot at the end. This would tap constantly on the window, driving people mad.

Quite a few characters lived on Honeywell. Walt Rounds had a Mynah bird that could say anything; it even *wolf-whistled* at the lasses as they walked past.

Outside the Keel Inn was an old barge, and as kids we used to fish off it. One day my brother Eric fell off into the water, and he might have drowned if a lad called Steve Rennison hadn't been around to pull him out. Steve had a calliper on his leg for years, but it didn't stop him coming to the rescue that day.

Our milk was delivered by a man with a horse and cart. The milkman would walk up the street delivering and collecting bottles, and he only had to whistle once and the horse (Major) would trudge up to where he was. Many times I would get a bucket and shovel and follow them up the street, collecting the manure for dad's garden.

To celebrate the Queen's Silver Jubilee, a party was organised for all the kids from Honeywell, Old Mill Lane and Bridge Street, but nearing party time, all the kids on Honeywell decided to hold their own celebrations. I asked the landlord of the Honeywell Inn if we could have our party in his pub, and he said yes. I bought a commemorative mug for all the kids, from the Symcox brothers, who had a business on Honeywell, and everyone had a great time.

Honeywell Inn 'Magnificent Seven'

When I married my wife Patricia in 1965, we moved into 35 Honeywell Street. At that time every house shared an outside toilet, and we shared with Mr. and Mrs Watson. It was very cold in the winter and the only toilet paper we had was the Daily Herald or Sheffield Green Un, cut up into little squares, and hung on a nail behind the toilet door.

We did our bit to make the house nice, adding new wooden windows and re-pointing. We were also the first to fit a new inside toilet and bathroom.

Quite a few men who lived on Honeywell worked at the pit, usually at Carlton, Woolley, North Gawber, Monk Bretton, Dodworth or Barnsley Main. A man called Wally was the knocker up, and would come around the street at 4 a.m., rattling the bedroom windows with a long cane which had wires fastened on the end. The men had to get out of bed and let him see they were up before he would move to the next house. He would continue knocking until they answered him.

One day a lad who was courting George White's sister was in the Honeywell Inn, and asked Wally if he would knock him up. "Of course," Wally said, and asked where the lad lived. "Birdwell" was the reply. "I'll have to hop on mi bike then," Wally replied.

The Honeywell Inn was a regular place for everybody from around the area to meet up; we had a darts team that won Pogmoor League, year in, year out. We also won a competition run by Sheffield Star newspaper called Magnificent Seven. The prize was £100 plus one hundred pints, which in those days was fantastic. I was the non-playing captain who put the team together; we had ten players registered, and seven to play.

There were also many great trips organised by the darts team, such as one to see the Scotland Ayr Gold Cup and to Jersey.

Allan Micklethwaite had a greyhound and raced it at the Dillington Dog Track a few times, but unfortunately it never won a race. However, it did break into his pigeon loft, killing and eating some of his prize homing birds. Another of the sporting events held was pigeon racing in the Keel field, when dedicated men trained and raced *milers* every Sunday at 11am.

THE THINGS WE USED TO DO
Graham Holt

I lived in Canal Street from being born until 1969, when the family moved to the Locke Park area. I have many memories of living down there, lots of them good and not many bad, with my mates Sevvy, Steph, Nocker Short, Ginna Kerr, Big Shaun and Little Shaun just to name a few.

We used to spend hours *laiking* in the Keel field and Doc's field (Dockerty's). During school holidays we spent hours at Willow Bank, swimming in the *bomb-oyle* on the River Dearne. One of the highlights of the summer on Saturday and Sunday afternoons was watching the *big uns,* as we called them, trying to walk the pipe across the *cut* outside the Keel pub, a lot of them drunk – there was many a ruined suit and shirt.

Another big thing was Bonfire Night. We used to start collecting *bunny wood* round about the end of September, going to Tom Roberts' haulage yard for old lorry tyres (sorry about adding to the demise of the ozone layer, but we didn't know any better then).

The old empty houses on Milton Street and William Street were a good source of entertainment, playing with gas masks from the war and seeing who could collect the most keys. I always remember when they pulled the houses down; it was brilliant watching them turn into a pile of rubble, even though it was where my uncle's family and my granddad lived for years.

My dad worked at the '*Nail Oyle'* and started there when he was fourteen, when he left school in 1943. He says it used to belong to two brothers called Cyril and Ken Waring and was officially called Dockworks, Canal Street.

I always remember the time my cousin *Arfa*, real name Arthur, rolled a tyre down the Keel field and it went straight through the rear window of the Keel. Harry Palmer, the landlord, went ape.... – what a laugh!

I started school at Beckett Street, but all I can remember is that there was a shelter at the top of the playground where we used to play when it was raining. *'What time is it Mr. Wolf?'* was one of the games. I also remember the toilets being outside and, being lads, we had competitions to see who could urinate the highest up the tiled wall. A bit crude I know, but highly amusing at the time.

I then went to Eldon Street School for about two years before I had to go to Wilthorpe Junior School. A bus was laid on to pick us up outside a shop on Honeywell Street. That was always a riot, loads of laughs - like a school trip every day.

I then went to Raley School, the first day in short *kecks* (trousers). I got *ribbed* all day by my big brother and his mates – didn't make that mistake again! I also got threatened to get chucked down the bank into a bed of nettles - apparently this was your welcome to Raley! I ducked and dived all week.

When I look back the teachers were brilliant; the majority of male teachers were ex-forces and laid down strict rules, not like the liberal *do-gooders* of today. The teachers I remember are Miss Marsh (Geography), Mr. Hitchen (English), Mr. Bennett (Physics/Chemistry), Mr. Walton (Art), Mr. Bostwick (Maths/Games) and the headmaster Mr. Jones. The most feared female teacher was Fanny Garbutt, a four foot ten inch Welsh demon!

'The Keel Inn' (Tasker Trust)

CHILDHOOD MEMORIES
Elaine Jackson

I was born in 1946 and until I was 14 I lived on Honeywell Street. In 1972 I came back to live on Honeywell Street with my husband and daughter, and am still here.

As a child I attended Beckett Street Infant School, and my only memory from those days was the afternoon nap we had to take. We all had a camp bed and a little grey blanket; each of us had a different motif on our blanket and kept that blanket while we were there. I seem to remember my motif being a sailboat.

I went from there to Eldon Street Junior School. Mr. Aveyard was Headmaster; other teachers I remember were Mr. Esplain, Mrs Moore and Mrs Trigg. Mrs Trigg was the fourth year teacher and one of the things she taught us was *'joined up writing.'* I enjoyed those lessons, but, unfortunately, over the years my handwriting has deteriorated. Mrs Trigg would not be happy.

Elaine and Linda Fidler

Elaine and Linda FidlerI passed the Eleven Plus exam, and went on to Barnsley Girls High School. The uniform was a grey skirt, (gymslip for the first year), white blouse, red tie and a grey blazer and beret. There was a strict uniform policy (even down to the grey knickers). Berets had to be worn when going to and from school (being seen without it would result in a report and three reports meant detention). In the first year we wore the beret correctly, but as the years went on, we clipped it further and further back on our heads until it couldn't be seen from the front.

After leaving the High School at 16, I went to work as a Cadet Nurse at Beckett Hospital. It was a great way to find out if you were cut out for nursing. It was hard work for £16 per month, but we did learn basic nursing care such as bed bathing, as well as all the cleaning jobs we had to do, washing and polishing curtain rails and cleaning the sluice room (believe it or not, two cadets cleaning the sluice room could have a lot of fun). I carried on with my nurse training at Beckett and St Helen's Hospitals, qualifying in 1967. In those days we looked like nurses, in pristine uniforms with crisp white hats and aprons. When we qualified as Staff Nurses, we were proud to wear our deep mauve uniform, and especially our silver buckles. I went on to become a Night Sister and continued nursing in Barnsley until my retirement.

My childhood on Honeywell Street was happy and free. We could roam anywhere. A few of us would get on our bikes and take off for the day; our parents never had to worry about us, (it would be a different story today). We would go to Tinker's Pond or down to the *'cut'* (the canal) to fish for sticklebacks. We played *kick can, sticks* or *nipsy* on the *'backs'* or climbed the high wall into the *'big yard'* (the back of Bridge Street). For several years this is where a bonfire was held on November 5th, and everyone joined in with jacket potatoes, toffee and Parkin.

In 1953, few people had a television, so for the Coronation of the Queen, most of the street piled into the only house that had one. I remember our first television, a tall cabinet with a tiny screen and only one channel.

My aunt and uncle lived in Old Mill Lane. When my older sister started work, I took over my aunt's weekly shopping. I would collect her shopping list and go to the Co-op on the corner of Beckett Street and Eldon Street. It was a typical old-fashioned shop with all the drawers behind the high counter. I didn't get paid each week, but my aunt paid into the *'Three-and-a-half-penny'* club at Pickersgill's shop (now Dot's), and in December I would get some of the half-pennies, in all about £7, a lot of money in those days.

Unfortunately, I have few photographs of my childhood but remember those days affectionately.

Since losing my husband, I have made new friends by joining different groups in the Honeywell area, and I am living a very full and busy life. Would I have had that if I had lived anywhere else? For me it has been a very friendly place.

'Beckett Hospital Prize Giving' 1968 Elaine Fidler, third from right
front row

GROWING-UP IN HONEYWELL
Elaine Miller (nee Holmes)

In the 1930's, my dad George Holmes met my mum, Edith Caborn at Barnsley Baths. Dad lived on Honeywell Street, and mum lived on Honeywell Lane. They eventually married and moved into a house on Honeywell Grove, and that is where my brother Geoff and I were born.

My childhood friend was Brenda Frost. She lived two doors up from my grandma in Honeywell Lane. We all used to get whips and tops for 'Pancake Day' and then we would compete to see who could chalk the best pattern on the top.

On Sunday afternoons, Brenda and I used to get a bottle of water, and some jam sandwiches and go for a picnic in farmer Wright's field. After school on Thursday, it was my job to go to the Co-op, where Mr. Pickles was the manager, to collect mum's shopping order for the week. I still have her order book.

A typical order would be:

Vegetable 14
1/4lb 99 Tea 8
2" Sugar 7
1" Lard 9
1" Marg 10
H.P. Beans 4
Tin Pears 10
" Pineapple 6
Small Dairy Cream 4
1lb Icing Sugar 6
Biscuits 6
Large Daz 1 6
Toilet Soap 8
Toilet Rolls 7½
Vim 6½
Flakes 3
2 boxes matches 3
20 Park Drives 2 4
1.5 2

1/4lb 99 Tea 0 8
2" Sugar 0 7
1" Lard 0 9
1" Marg 1 4
1lb Golden Syrup 0 9
H.P. Beans 0 4
Tin Kidney Beans 0 6
Fruit Salad 1 2
Gravy Salt 0 3
2lb Dates 0 4½
3" Be-to S.R. 11
Small Dairy Cream
1lb Fairy Soap 1 0
Fairy Liquid 1 4
Stardrops 0 6
Shampoo 0 5
Biscuits 1 2½
2 boxes matches 0 3
20 Park Drives 2 4
Paid £1.62

Co-op Grocery Book

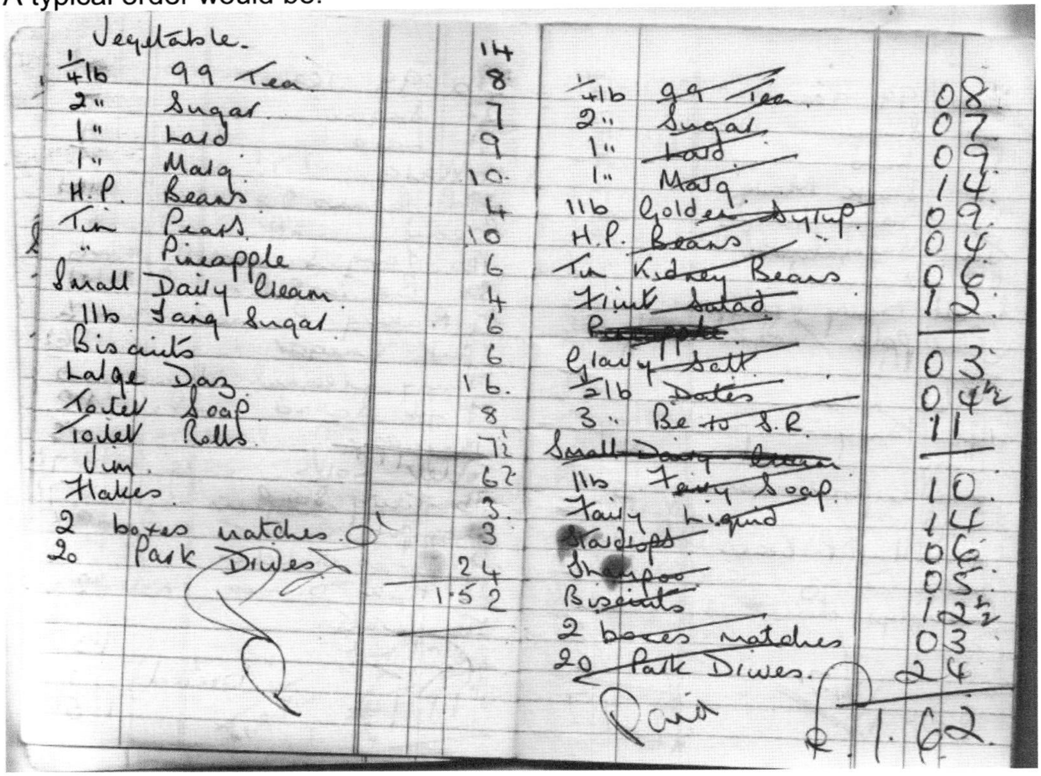

On a Sunday morning, I would *don* my best clothes and go to St Barnabas Church, with Mrs Bedford who lived next door.

The highlight of the year for me was the big bonfire that we used to have on the hill, across the road from where we lived. For most of the summer holidays we would go out collecting wood for the fire; this was called *bunny wooding*. All the mums used to make something to eat, ready for the big day. Mr. Rushton, who lived on the Grove, used to come walking up through the field dressed as 'Father Christmas,' bringing all the children some fireworks.

Each week I used to go to my grandma's house and scrub her steps. For this she

Edith & George Holmes

would give me an empty pop bottle to take back to the off-license. In exchange for the bottle, we would get money back and then we would call at Smith's Fish and Chip shop for a bag of chips.

All of my memories of living in Honeywell are good ones. People were so friendly, just like a big happy family. I will never forget those days.

Elaine Holmes & Brenda Frost

MY EARLY CHILDHOOD (An extract from an autobiography)
Alan Gothard

My first memories include attending Beckett Street Infants School from the age of four years, being quite young relative to most of the class. Whilst there I recall (strangely) being invited to have a nap on the camp beds provided mid-afternoon. Also, I remember the freezing outside toilets to which one had to venture in winter. I must have done reasonably well, because when I transferred to Eldon Street Junior School at the age of seven years old, I was placed in a class "a year above my age." Whilst this sounds good, it meant leaving one's friends behind and joining a strange class. To add to my consternation, my father always took us on holiday for the first two weeks in September, meaning I was late starting. I recall joining the class of Mr. Sykes and that they were doing long division which I hadn't a clue about. I soon settled, however, and Mr. Sykes appointed me *Keeper of the Slipper*. When anyone misbehaved, I was asked for the slipper, which was then used on the rear end of miscreants. This seemed to be a period when I was eternally repairing my own trousers with patches which then proceeded to come loose. I remember walking home sideways; keeping the large hole against the wall so no one could see my rear.

Other Eldon Street School memories include being entrusted with a message to take to another class. When I got there, I'd completely forgotten the message! This was a typical example of what my grandmother termed the *absent minded professor* behaviour. I was bullied mercilessly at this school by one particular boy; I was followed every evening going home and given a 'going over.' His activities only ceased when elder brother Colin intercepted him and I believe put him in a bin! Imagine doing that today. The Headmaster was Mr. Aveyard and two of the teachers that I recall were Mrs Moore and Mrs Twigg. The former was someone to beware of, as she was known to work her way along a queue of children smacking legs! Mrs Twigg was very well respected by the children. I recall us being spell-bound as she would read Huckleberry Finn and Tom Sawyer; you could hear a pin drop in the class. When she was taken ill, some of us visited her, unannounced, at her Laithes Lane home and were made very welcome, being shown a blackbird's nest with chicks in her rear hedge!

Whilst at Eldon Street School, I had my first and only lead role in a theatrical production. This was titled 'The Three Tassels' and I now haven't a clue what the plot was. I *starred* opposite Elaine Senior, also from Eaming View. At playtime we had epic football matches, with a tennis ball, in the sloping playground and I recall being in the school football team and playing matches on the ground behind the Toll Bar pub, at the very bottom of Eldon Street and also on the Redfearns ground behind our house. My father

Alan Gothard

watched this latter match, which made me a little nervous. Afterwards, I asked him what he thought and he said, "Tha played like a teacake," leaving me somewhat crushed!

After four years at primary school it was time for the dreaded Eleven Plus examinations. When the results became available, the whole school was mustered in assembly and there were two boys to go to the Barnsley & District Grammar School for Boys and two girls to the High School for Girls. I recall the ripple that went around the children when my name was announced for the grammar school. Others went to vocational schools and the rest to Raley Secondary School.

Leaving aside school, the area that I was brought up in seemed to be one big pleasure park to us kids. Not twenty yards from the front door was the canal, offering endless possibilities for fun and games. To the right (north), the Barnsley Canal tow-path went past Old Mill glassworks, by the pool where barges would tie up in earlier days to supply the town's needs; then past the paper mill, facing across to Keel Field, (where my father's grandmother had a gypsy caravan apparently!), passing under various hump-backed bridges. These bridges allowed the horses pulling the barges to transfer from bank to bank as needed. This was before my time unfortunately. At a bend in the canal was the nail factory, a remnant of earlier industry in the area. It was here that we caught a pike, which was a bit of a handful to handle. I also remember this bend in winter when it was iced over. We children were playing on the ice when one boy went through, his face appearing under the ice whilst we peered down at him. Thankfully, he got out and I recall being struck that he was more concerned that he would "get it in the neck" for his wet clothing rather than nearly losing his life! Then on for a few miles to the Thirty-Two Steps, a foot bridge over the canal which led up a steep hill to Tinkers Pond. This was a deep pool, quite dangerous, having steep banks.

To the left (south) from our house, the Barnsley Canal arrived at a T-junction after about a mile, bearing left, across a magnificent aqueduct that carried the canal over the River Dearne and the railway, and onwards, via a lock, to Cudworth, on its way to join the Calder and thence to the Humber Estuary, allowing coal to be taken out of Barnsley.

THE WILLOW
Garry Smythe (formerly known as Garry Broadhead)

I was born in 1953 and for the first eight years of my life lived down a little street off Smithies Lane called Pleasant View Street - aptly named. I moved to Wombwell when my parents divorced, but as my wife would confirm, I have always referred to my Pleasant View address as home.

We lived at number 6, the third one from the top of maybe thirty to forty small two up, two down, terraced houses. My grandparents lived near the bottom; an uncle lived at the very bottom house, with two further uncles living on the same street. Mr. and Mrs Parkes lived at the top house, and their two youngest children were my close friends, along with a young girl called Linda Micklethwaite. The street backed onto the *Willow*, a mystical place to a young lad, with the tall wild ferns and wild flowers making great dens. I remember the old

'Tinkers Pond' (Tasker Trust)

sunken barges on the canal, which brings back memories of me pulling out a young Glenn Parkes whilst up to the neck myself, only to return home to be scolded and my backside smacked for going near the canal, before having the chance to explain. It was only when Mrs Parkes came to my mother and told her that I had "saved her son's life" (women have the need to exaggerate), that I was duly praised.

The happy hours I spent there, our walks to Eldon Street School when we used to set off from the junction of Rockingham Street and Smithies Lane at the same time as the bus, and run to school in an attempt to beat it. Picnics spent with my mother and many borrowed kids, from more than willing neighbours, in the splendour of the Willow. I've told my son and daughter many, many times about this magical area, so much so that I've even told them to scatter my ashes there when the time comes.

In the summer we would take the long walk to Tinkers Pond, which would be full of local tourists. I remember the tales of the old crumbling house near Tinkers Pond, with its ghosts and such, enough to make us venture there in gangs but never alone. I remember the Kenny family, many kids, not so well off, but honest, reliable, down to earth.

I have been told that my grandfather's brother, a member of the Wright family, did in fact own all the land to the right of Rockingham Street that now houses an entire estate and a pub. My mother worked at Ceag in town, making light bulbs for houses and cars alike.

I remember the Co-op on the hill, going there with my mother for her *divi*. Many years later, my uncle bought the shop at the top of Pleasant View, and another uncle rented a barn at the top, to use as storage for his mobile grocery business.

Yes indeed many, many memories of a truly pleasant area.

THE INGHAMS OF HONEYWELL
Eric Bailey

In 1891, George and Martha Ingham lived at 33 New Bridge Street, Barnsley with seven- month old Emily. They moved to Clanricarde Street in 1894. William was one of nine children born to George and Martha around that time. William married Elsie Simpson and they lived at 5 William Street, Honeywell in 1917. They had four children; Alfred, Arthur, James and Rosella.

Betty Ingham

Arthur met Gladys Kirk, where she worked, at the Prince of Wales public house (at the junction of Eldon Street and Old Mill Lane). They married on 4th July 1942 at St. John's Church, Darfield Road, Cudworth, and lived with Arthur's parents at William Street for a number of years. They had two daughters whilst living there, named Margaret and Betty (my wife), born 1943 and 1944 respectively, followed by Michael. Arthur worked at Barnsley Main Colliery after leaving school and later at Houghton Main Colliery.

Arthur's brother, Alfred, went to Grove Street School, after which he became a plasterer at Kexborough. Alfred married Jane, and went to live with her at 21 William Street, Honeywell. He joined 2nd Battalion, West Yorkshire Regiment (Prince of Wales' Own), the Army's First Militia in 1939, subsequently serving in Iceland. He had a narrow escape from death, being one of four survivors, when eighteen men were drowned at sea, during a gale.

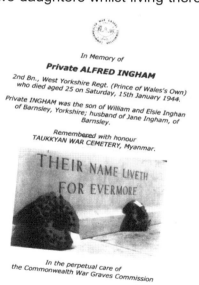

In Memory of
Private ALFRED INGHAM
2nd Bn., West Yorkshire Regt. (Prince of Wales's Own) who died aged 25 on Saturday, 15th January 1944.
Private INGHAM was the son of William and Elsie Ingham of Barnsley, Yorkshire; husband of Jane Ingham, of Barnsley.
Remembered with honour
TAUKKYAN WAR CEMETERY, Myanmar.

THEIR NAME LIVETH FOR EVERMORE

In the perpetual care of the Commonwealth War Graves Commission

He was sent to serve in India in 1943 where he had two or three spells in hospital. The last letter written by Alfred was received by Jane in December of that year. Alfred was killed in action whilst serving in the Indian theatre of war, aged twenty-five years, on Saturday, 15th January 1944. Private Alfred Ingham is remembered with honour at TAUKKYAN WAR CEMETERY, Myanmar in the perpetual care of the Commonwealth War Graves Commission ('Their Name Liveth for Evermore').

THE WAR AND HONEYWELL
Violet Booth

In 1941 when I was nineteen, I volunteered to join the army (ATS), and my sister Isabella was conscripted into the same regiment one month later. The work I chose to do was in the catering section, where I had to help prepare and serve food for the officers and other personnel, plus help out at special functions and events. For this I was paid approximately fourteen shillings per week, although what I received was about nine shillings because the rest was paid as a pension to my mum.

When we learned we were to be transferred from Pontefract to either Barnsley or Leeds, my friend, another cook, and I prayed it would be Leeds because neither of us had ever heard of Barnsley. Our commanding officer was aware of this, so once she knew it was going to be Barnsley, she drove us through from Pontefract to show us where we would be stationed. I was very fortunate to be billeted along with others in a small bungalow very near St Mary's Church and the Chronicle office, which was nice.

The entire regiment was accommodated in various places around town, mostly in private houses and public halls. The women were placed in and around Victoria Road whilst a lot of the men were settled in the Arcadian Hall, which was also where I worked, providing cooked meals, sandwiches and snacks for one hundred and eighty service men and women.

It was not an easy job, particularly due to the rationing of food that affected us all. I had to work around all this and was still expected to provide a good nourishing meal every day of the week that was not too boring. Creating new menus was sometimes a nightmare. However, because I was good at what I did, I soon rose in my unit to become a corporal.

The servicemen's area of work was mostly to do with transport, whilst servicewomen were almost always either clerical workers or drivers for the officers.

After a few months, the Mayor Mr Truman, issued an open invitation to any serviceman/woman to come to tea and then be given a guided tour of the Town Hall. It was a lovely day and we enjoyed it very much; the Mayor was very appreciative of the work the services were doing.

We had a very strict curfew and men were not allowed anywhere near our billet. We couldn't go out at all on Monday which was our utility day, a day we had to catch up with all our washing, ironing, shoe cleaning etc.

On June 6th 1943, my day off, I met the man who was to become my husband Richard (Dick) Booth. It was my sister's birthday and she persuaded me and a friend to go for a port and lemon at the Corner Pin to help her celebrate. We were having a laugh and enjoying our drink when Dick walked in; his mother usually came with him but this day he said she was a bit upset and didn't want to come. She had found out he had been chased earlier by the police for playing *toss-a-halfpenny* in the Keel field.

Anyway, he had a drink with us and because he lived in the same direction, walked back with us to our billet. He told me he was a miner and worked at Redbrook pit. Well I didn't want to marry a miner so I decided to 'stand him up' on our first date; however, later that evening I bumped into him and we went for a walk. He took me to Honeywell and introduced me to his cousins who lived on John Edward Street; there were so many of them I thought the whole area must be related. After that, we walked through the Keel field down towards the canal which I was not thrilled about. I don't like water and I was worried what Dick's intentions were; I remember thinking, "What am I doing here with a man I didn't know? He might try to drown me or something."

Well he didn't, and we were eventually married in 1944, and went to live with his aunt, Mrs Gibson, at 116 Honeywell Street. She had just been notified that two of her three sons had been killed on active service; the third one was discharged on compassionate grounds and sent home.

After renting number 86 Honeywell Street for a while, we asked the landlord if we could buy the house. Surprisingly it was granted, and we set about making improvements to our property. The first job was to panel the front door, and then we removed the black leaded fireplace and replaced it with a modern tiled one. The stone sink and set pot (boiler) were taken out and replaced with modern units, but best of all, the stone stairs had stair rods fitted so they could be carpeted. The house was lovely and we stayed there sixteen years; our son Richard was born in 1945 and our family was complete.

I was discharged from the army when they found out I was pregnant, which suited Dick and me because my unit had been posted to Kent.

Our house cost us two hundred pounds when we bought it, and we were able to sell for four hundred, so we made a small profit and moved to Mottram Street in 1960/61 where we lived until ten years ago. Mavis Gibbs was the girl who bought my house on Honeywell Street and we soon became very good friends. We did lots of things together and along with other people arranged coffee mornings, shopping trips, taking the kids to school etc.

We also enjoyed being part of Saint Barnabas's Church, where Richard (our son) and I were confirmed together. I did various things to help with church funds like jumble sales, cake stalls, bric-a-brac, flower arranging etc. My friends and I also liked to go to the whist drives which were held at the church every Thursday.

Our evening entertainment was usually at the Harborough Hills Working Men's Club. We have had many wonderful times taking part in all the various competitions like fancy dress and Easter bonnet parades, May day events, New Year and Christmas parties; the list is endless.

The Honeywell Inn used to have nights when people would get up and sing, much like a karaoke night now. The singer would do their particular song and if it was good, customers would throw money to them, usually just a few coppers. The money that was collected was not for the performer; it was saved and sent on to the troops who were away fighting. One night I only had

Violet with her medals

three halfpennies so I threw them, but instead of landing on the floor they ended up in the landlord's pint on the bar. Everyone laughed, shouting, "Bet you can't do that again!"

Looking back, our time spent in the Honeywell area, sharing our lives with family and friends, was special. We enjoyed the friendship of each other and we knew we could rely on them if needed. I remember one night in particular; it was around two in the morning and my husband Dick was rolling around in pain. I didn't know what to do and no one had a telephone in those days. Looking out of my window, I saw a light on in my neighbour's (Walt Rounds) house, so I ran and banged on the door. He and his son very quickly went out to fetch Doctor Thackeray, who came with his suit on over the top of his pyjamas. He diagnosed acute appendicitis and Dick was admitted at once to Barnsley hospital. I shall always be grateful to them for their thoughtfulness and quick action.

After sixty-six years of marriage, Dick and I are still happy and content with our lives, and have many precious memories of Honeywell and the folk who lived there.

Footnote: *Since this story was written, Dick has sadly passed away. We want to pass on our condolences to Violet and their son Richard; however Dick did get to read their story, so we hope it will offer some comfort to Violet to see her account of their happy life together in print.*

1946
Margaret Ferry

It was a Saturday and must have been summer, because it was warm and sunny and I was wearing a dress and sandals. My granddad was taking me with him to have his haircut. We went through the ginnel on Denton Street, by the Co-op on the corner of Beckett Street and Eldon Street. Up Eldon Street, across to the paper shop (sweets!), and on to Bridge Street to the penny barber. Lads were sitting on the doorsteps of the houses we passed. They wore short trousers, and sandals; some wore singlets, knitted by hand.

There was a queue at the barbers and all the haircuts were the same – short back and sides! I remember watching a game of marbles whilst we waited and granddad placed a bet whilst he was having his hair cut - I know about the bet because I was told not to say anything, but if he was lucky I could have an ice cream. On the way home, I remember stopping to admire my sandals – they were red – and granddad said when the dray horses went up Eldon Street on Sunday he was going to collect the droppings and put them in my sandals to help me grow!

HAPPY DAYS
Cynthia Brown

I lived in Redfearn Street, which was divided into two yards, with a large air-raid shelter in the middle. My friends and I used to go inside and dress up and put little shows on, and then our parents and neighbours would sit and watch.

My Aunt Winnie and Uncle Bill lived in the bottom yard; they had seven children. We played together, and when it was any of their birthdays, Uncle Bill's brother, who owned Palfreyman's ice cream factory, situated on a small street between Eldon Street and Old Mill Lane, would bring large tubs of his ice cream. It was the best in Barnsley. I think it closed in the 60's.My Grandma lived in Canal Street, and her local pub was the Keel Inn. It was very small in those days. In the field at the side was an old authentic gypsy caravan, where Gypsy Rhia lived. She was friendly with my Gran and I was allowed to go inside. It was very beautiful, with lovely ornaments. She lived many years in her caravan, near the pub and canal

Artist 'Andy Phillips' impression of 'Gypsy Rhia' and her caravan

'THE REAL MR. COOL'
Sid Williams

Mr. W. Palfreyman was the Honeywell Ice-Cream man from around 1945-75. His dairy was at the rear of Honeywell Street, in a little alleyway that ran between Old Mill Lane and Eldon Street North.

In the beginning he worked with a horse and cart, but later went on to Bradford Jowitt Vans.
The horse, which was really a mule, was called 'Sandy,' and yes, you are right, it was ginger. Sandy the mule came from Lundwood, and his owner was a man called Clifford, who lived at Cundy Cross.

My friend, Eric Symcox, used to walk to Lundwood every weekend to fetch the mule. He would walk miles, if it meant he got a ride on a horse. When Mr. Palfreyman had finished on Sunday night, Eric would take 'Sandy' back to Lundwood.

I, myself, worked at Palfreyman's Ices, so did Eric's brother Dennis Symcox, and if I remember rightly, so did Mr. Bill Exley, who lived in Old Mill Lane, opposite the backs that link Old Mill Lane and Eldon Street North.

Back then, you could not order a '99' cone (a cone with a chocolate flake), your choice was a twopenny or fourpenny cone, or you could take a basin and get 2-3 scoops. 'Happy Days.'

Dennis Symcox

THE BEST ICE CREAM EVER'
Elaine Jackson

Palfreyman's ice cream was the best in Barnsley, and the great thing about living on Honeywell Street, was that instead of waiting for an ice cream van we could go straight to the factory. The ice cream factory was at the top of the steps on the lane between Eldon Street and Old Mill Lane, behind Honeywell Street.

On special occasions we would go to the factory with a basin and have it filled with scoops of their delicious ice cream.

Palfreyman's was still there when we left Honeywell Street in 1960, unfortunately it was no longer there when I returned with my own family in 1972.

You cannot get ice cream as good as that was anywhere in Barnsley these days.

THE GARDEN HOUSE
Gloria Hesford (nee Phillips)

Artist impression of 'Garden House' Honeywell Street

Back in the early 1950's my family moved into 101 Honeywell Street, better known to *Honeywellers* as *The Garden House*. It had always been my dad's dream to live there, and at last the opportunity had presented itself. Dad's grandparent's family had moved to Barnsley from Staffordshire in the early 1890's, maybe seeking work; they lived in two houses, numbers 11 and 17 Clanricarde Street.

After my grandparents, Thomas Phillips and Annie Hall were married in 1905; they moved into 112 Honeywell Street and stayed there all their married life. Their children were all born in that house, including my dad Tommy, born 20 January 1920.

They were a big family that moved together from Staffordshire, and when they all eventually got married and had children of their own, most of them stayed, living in and around Honeywell. When I was young we had so many relations living in the area, it was like going home when we visited.

Unfortunately I never knew either of my grandparents because they were dead before I was born, but hearing the stories my dad and others told about their lives in Honeywell, made me think it must be a special place.

During the war Tommy (dad) joined the RAF, and although I don't think he saw much active service, he was demobbed with a bad injury to his hip and leg, caused by two accidents he had. The first, whilst re-fuelling an aeroplane and the second while home on leave. These injuries left him with a very bad limp, and other health problems, which in turn limited his job prospects; however this did not stop him providing for his family.

Our family during the Garden House years consisted of Mum, Dad and five children, all under the age of ten, and I can say we weren't too eager to move to Honeywell. We were used to the comfort of our three-bedroomed council house in Lundwood, with its added luxury of hot water and a bathroom; we also had friends we didn't want to leave behind and I loved Littleworth School.

However, we were used to change, particularly around the house, as dad bought and sold things all the time in order to keep the family going; a favourite saying of mum's was that she never got to polish a piece of furniture twice. Anyhow, all of us would have followed my dad to the end of the earth, and this move looked like being a big adventure, so it happened and dad's dream came true. We swapped houses with Mrs Armin, who lived in the Garden House, and I know that 56 years later she still lives in our old house in Lundwood.

I don't know the 'ins and outs' of it all because I was only eight years old at the time, but I do remember all the fuss, the scrimping and scraping my parents had to do in order to make the move happen. I had recently been bought a lovely little piano because they thought I showed talent, but even that had to go.

Dad was in his element and loved being back home in Honeywell, and because the house was in an allotment, he was able to keep hens and grow his own vegetables. He also bought a horse and cart which he used for various things like selling firewood, house clearances etc.

We always had an open house and people would drop in any time of the day, so there weren't many dull moments. I remember at the bottom of the garden were some sheds where dad stabled the horse, and after it had been groomed every night he and a few of his friends, including uncles and cousins, would be in the other shed chopping firewood to sell. The atmosphere was great because they would have the radio on loud, sometimes late into the evening; they would be laughing, singing and telling jokes. Mum would be ferrying cups of tea and buns about, especially if it had been baking day; everyone was made welcome and frequently dad would bring strangers home for tea.

Although my mum did everything she could to keep things pretty normal for us kids, it was not easy for her. She was always cooking, cleaning and generally falling in with my dad's plans for his next new adventure, so I can't say we had a 'run of the mill' childhood because we didn't, but what we did have was a lot of love.

The first winter we had in the Garden House was very cold; there were coal fires in the kitchen, and a small one in the lounge which we didn't really use. The water was heated in the 'set pot' (boiler) which was situated by the side of the kitchen range. We had to walk through the lounge to get to the stairs which in turn led to two bedrooms. I remember the very cold air which hit you when the door to the lounge was opened, but even worse than that was the outside toilet. Obviously, other arrangements were made for us kids to go to the toilet after dark. All this tells me how much mum must have loved my dad; we never, ever heard her complain about anything, she was cheerful all the time and never stopped singing.

Tommy Phillips (Dad)

As I said before, dad kept chickens and it was decided he would get an incubator. We kids had a quick lesson in biology, watching and waiting for new life to appear from the eggs; it was amazing for us to be part of all this, something most other kids wouldn't get to see unless they visited a farm. As the chicks hatched, my brothers and sister and I were each given one to look after. However, mine got sick when it was just a few days old. Mum tried hard to keep it alive; we stayed up all night, sitting beside the fire, the chick wrapped in cotton wool. Sadly, it died early that morning and we had a little funeral service, burying it just under the fence which ran along the pavement side of the garden, giving it a small grave with its own little cross which mum had made.

Along with the hens we had a beloved dog called Prince, a black and white collie with brown/black flecks on his paws. We dearly loved him and to us he was very much part of the family; however, he must have been a very unlucky dog because despite the lack of heavy traffic in 1954, Prince got killed on the road by a lorry. It was a heartbreaking thing to happen so soon after we'd moved into the house; to say we were devastated is an understatement. We cried and cried and no amount of consoling could comfort us kids. He too was given a proper ceremony at his burial and was laid to rest beside my chick under the fence. When I'm on Honeywell Street now, I often go to that spot and remember; although houses have been built there I imagine I know just where they might be.

Anyway, a couple of weeks after this awful event, my dad came to Eldon Street School, at playtime to see myself and my brother and sister. He told us Prince had come back to life and was at home upstairs in the lobby, but we had to be careful not to let him out. That afternoon was so long - we couldn't wait for school to finish before we dashed home, as fast as our legs would carry us, and I remember the three of us bursting through the door, not even saying hello to mum in our eagerness to see the vision of loveliness that had happened. The big bedroom had a walk in lobby and we could hear scratching and whining, but we dare not open the door. Eventually we had to; I don't remember which one of us it was that plucked up the courage, but when the door was opened our beautiful Prince came bursting out jumping all over us and licking our faces. This dog was exactly the same as the one we'd lost; every marking on her was perfect, and we truly believed it was our beloved dog, come back to life. Remember, to us there was nothing my dad couldn't do, he even made miracles happen. It was some time later we were told this dog was in fact a bitch and her name was Floss, but for that short space of time we believed in miracles. Floss was a lovely dog with the same kind of temperament as Prince; we had her for many years and she was dearly loved.

We only spent one Christmas in the Garden House and my parents were very short of money, but mum always made the best of things. My dad had got her some new crockery in one of his 'flushed' moments, but it was looking as though this was going to have to be sold. It was Christmas Eve and had been snowing for days, so we older kids were out sledging. As it was getting dark we made our way home. When we walked through the door we were greeted with such a sight I have never been able to forget it. Because the lounge was so cold, mum kept a food cabinet in there which had a drop down leaf; as well as the food it also housed mum's new crockery. My two young brothers, John and Michael, had gone into the lounge while her back was turned and climbed up to get to the raisins she had for baking. One of them sat on the drop leaf and the cabinet toppled over; they were so lucky not to have been killed or at least badly hurt. When we came in the door, mum was

Doris Phillips (Mum)

trying to clean them up and both kids were crying. They stood there like two little Homepride men, with peaks of flour, sugar etc; on their heads. It was very upsetting, particularly for my mum, thinking how serious it could have been, but it was not long before we were all laughing because they looked so funny. I just wish we had had a camera. The lounge was a right mess and as you have probably guessed, the best crockery was also gone, most of it anyway.

Christmas was always special regardless of us not having much money (not many people did then). We never doubted Father Christmas would come, although other kids said there was no such person. I believed because I couldn't imagine how these gifts made their way to the bottom of our beds come Christmas morning, when our parents had no money. We could always be sure of an apple, orange, box of Maltesers, plus a small gift and a new penny; it was truly amazing and I feel so sad when young children today say they don't believe. Christmas morning would be spent playing with our toys and chasing Maltesers around the bedroom floor; they would roll everywhere because we had no carpets, only lino. That Christmas I got a doll. She was lovely, but over time her head came off; however, as I said before, my dad could do anything so there was no need to take her to the dolls' hospital. He could always mend her for me; he would stick the poker in the fire and when it was red and glowing, and because she was made of plastic, he would melt her neck and stick the head back in place. I remember the melted plastic smelled terrible.

She was repaired that often she did get to look awful, but she was mine and I would never part with her, so I just used to cover her neck up so other kids wouldn't laugh.

Dad liked a drink and many times when he was out with the horse after work, he would call at the Honeywell pub for a few pints. We always knew where he would be when the horse walked itself home. Sunday lunchtime he would go to the pub while mum made dinner. Afterwards he would come home very merry, throwing whatever change he had left in his pocket up in the air, there would be a mad scramble by any of us kids who were around to pick up what we could. We didn't get much because he didn't have much, but we always tried to make sure we were in when he came home. After lunch and a sleep, he would take the horse for its exercise down to the canal bank and give us and our friends a ride, bare back of course, no helmets; health and safety then was not an issue. I was a very popular friend to have on a Sunday.

I remember when Queen Elizabeth came to Barnsley in 1954; all school children were taken into town to watch her pass by. Our school didn't need to go far and I remember standing waving my flag on Eldon Street just before the bridge; all the traffic had been stopped but then my dad came through with the horse and cart. All the kids were waving their flags and cheering and I felt very proud. He told us later that, although a cordon was in place, the Queen was not expected for quite a while and he needed to get to the other side of town on business, so he managed to persuade the police to let him through.

Unfortunately our cottage was condemned by the council and became part of a clearance order in 1955. Once again we were on the move, this time to Athersley North. Although my dad's dream lasted only a short time, at least he experienced it and I look back on our time in Honeywell with love and affection. I am sure we all learned that money is not everything in life, love is. If you care enough you can cope with most things. When we moved to Athersley my mum had another four children, my three brothers and a sister. They know nothing of our time in Honeywell and I can't help but feel they missed so much.

HONEYWELL CHILDCARE HOME (1955)
Jan Sefton

I was small, the house was huge; that was my first thought when I went into care. I was put into what was known in the home as *the ballroom,* and there I met my new *aunties* - these were the women who would look after me. They were to decide what I ate, what I wore, what time I went to bed and what time I got up.

I was scrubbed clean and kitted out, and then I was given a long list of do's and don'ts. Later, I met my housemates, gathered from all over the Barnsley area for all kinds of reasons; then I realised they were all boys.

There were two adjoining houses back then, Georgeville for the boys and Maryville for the girls. Boys and girls were kept separate, but, because I had been placed in care with my baby brother, I was allowed to stay in the boys' house, and I became the biggest tomboy of all.

I soon settled into the routine - a cooked breakfast every morning and a cooked tea when we came back from school. Every Sunday we were marched off to church; we went to St Barnabas for mass, then in the afternoon we went back again for Sunday school.

Saturday was the best time of the week because my dad came to take us out. He tried desperately to keep us at home whilst working at Woolley Colliery, but failed. After he died, I found receipts for the money he had paid each week to keep us in care. Every Saturday he took us into town, we went around the stalls or to the cinema. Peas and pies were next at Oldfield's caravan in the market place.

There were problems with being in care. If food was put before you, it had to be eaten; if you didn't like fatty meat - hard luck! One cold night I kept my vest on for bed, something that was not allowed. The *auntie* on duty that night noticed it, "you're wearing a vest in bed" she accused. I denied it and was slapped hard, not, however, for wearing the vest but for lying.

Despite the blips and wanting my dad to be there all the time, I wasn't unhappy. We were kept clean, well fed and no one gave us a bad time out of the house; we were a formidable bunch together. For more years than I care to remember, Honeywell was my home; it was not by choice but it could have been much worse. We were taught lessons most children would never know - we learned not to show fear or our emotions.

When the rooms of Maryville and Georgeville were finally emptied, I would think there was the echo of a thousand sighs.

MARYVILLE CHILDREN'S HOME
Trevor Clarke

I lived in Maryville children's home (now there's a chapter in itself) on Rockingham Street for about five years up to about 1959. The building was split into two houses - Maryville and Georgeville. Maryville was run by two ladies: the matron, Aunty Alice (Alice Durkin) and Aunty Dorothy (Dorothy Banks). Alice Durkin spent most of her working life at Maryville. I believe her sister was Mary Brannan who lived at Carrington Avenue near Raley school, and who was Barnsley's first lady Mayor. I attended Beckett Street Infants where the headmistress was Miss Foundier (later Mrs Barnes) and also St Barnabas Church on Old Mill Lane. I then moved to Eldon Street Juniors and was in Mrs Moore's class. I remember at Eldon Street Juniors, you always knew when it was dinner time because the siren at the Star Paper Mill would run for a whole minute at midday. It was very loud; I bet it could be heard all over Barnsley (they wouldn't get away with it today).

Another memory, is being taken out onto the pavement in front of the school one February day in 1958, to watch the funeral cortege of Tommy Taylor, who had been killed in the Munich air crash, pass by on its way to Monk Bretton church for burial. I remember white being significant, either a white coffin or a white hearse, I can't remember which.

Whenever I see the name Cherryholme I always think of Honeywell Street. Christopher Cherryholme was in my class, and I remember the remarks made by the teachers at the length of his name when they had to write it out on the blackboard; (and I just found out why!)

'OH DEAR THOSE BRACES'
John Stephen Taylor

It was 1943, and of course there was a war on with all its worries, partings, anxieties and heartaches. Daily newspapers were full of war information and photos. I remember carrying the gas mask to school and back home, and being constantly reminded not to forget it. However, at three years old, we really didn't know how serious the situation we were living through was. On and around Honeywell Street there was quite a gang of us, born between 1939 and 1941, so we were never short of playmates.

My personal memories of the years from 1942 onward become more vivid as the years go by, so my story, connected with the braces, is a personal tale, true, but should not be read if one has just eaten. I know that although it's my own story, many others trod the same path - all because of those braces!

These leather braces fastened to six buttons on the trousers, and I remember my mother attaching them, and at the same time coming out with some choice words as she struggled like hell to manoeuvre the tough leather over the buttons. On top of the vest and shirt would be the braces, followed by a wool sweater, home knitted with love.

Well, shortly after dinner at Beckett Street Infant School, we were instructed to go and collect our little fold-up beds (made from lightweight tubular steel and canvas), pick up a blanket and lay down for a while, so that we could be off our feet, and encouraged to sleep. This, from memory, became giggle time, and we were often reprimanded by our teacher, who constantly instructed us to close our eyes. This ruling applied to us because of our age, and the need to rest for a while.

One day, after the rest period, and having taken my bed and blanket back to where they were stored, I felt the need to visit the toilet. I walked up to our teacher and asked, "Please can I go to the lav?" 'We don't say that!' was the reply, so I correctly asked, "Please Miss, may I leave the room?" The short walk to the toilet block across the yard seemed a long way and the trauma of the next few minutes I can hardly describe. As I stood there, at three years and a few months old, struggling to release the uncompromising leather braces over the buttons, I knew that I wasn't going to win, and as desperation and panic took over, the inevitable happened and I turned, in tears, and walked stiff-legged back to the classroom. I stood at the classroom door, the teacher looked around, and when she saw the mess, she just said three words; "You dirty fellow!" My three year old friends chorused and pointed, saying, "He's messed his sen!"

The dinner lady was given the job of walking me home, down Beckett Street, and along Honeywell Street to number 92. I heard a few sympathetic comments from neighbours as they saw my plight on the way home. The comments all said the same, "Poor little b........!"

It was Monday, and as everyone knows, Monday was always washday - dolly tub, peggy stick, rubbing board and carbolic soap. I was delivered to the back door where my mother was busy with the washing and as she looked down at my legs she said, "What the hell has tha done?" 'Dear, dear mam,' I must have thought what a question. Then it was luck all the way; well it would have been had it not been for the coal man and his wagon with a coal delivery. My mam, aware that the washing was complete, picked me up and stood me in the dolly tub (which was more than half full of hot soapy water), which felt comforting despite the strong smell of carbolic soap.

Then the coal man made his presence felt, when he shouted to my mother to take the washing in, off the line, to enable him to drive the coal wagon under the washing line to make a delivery further down the back yard. (Another way of assisting the coal man was for the housewife to use a sweeping brush to keep the line as high as possible, whilst the coal man reversed his wagon back up the yard, through the ginnel and out onto the road). This became a routine procedure and well appreciated by the coal wagon driver. I patiently waited in my temporary new home for my mam's return, and a few minutes later I was lifted out of the dolly tub, clean as a new pin, smelling of carbolic soap.

This kind of incident was common with children, till someone had a brainwave and decided that it would make life easier for us kids, if we wore our braces over the top of our jumpers. Then we could simply slip our braces over our shoulders and lower our short trousers.

Knowing that the problem had been solved, and confident that this sort of incident wouldn't happen again, and the dolly tub had been emptied, I joined my sister to eat Monday's dinner – *tatie 'ash*, followed by rice pudding. Oh, the smell and taste of the nutmeg! Happy times.

Artist 'Andy Phillips' impression of a 'Setpot'

WILTHORPE INFANTS SCHOOL
Katherine Symcox

Before going to Wilthorpe Infants' school, the nursery children were taken by train to Wakefield. What an adventure that must have been; it would have been the first time on a train for some of the little ones.

Mrs Valance, the head teacher, made the experience very exciting for the four year olds. They boarded the train in Barnsley and as they passed Woodstock

Road tunnel, the remainder of the nursery children were waiting to wave as the train passed by.

When the train got to Wakefield, the children were each given their third of a pint bottle of milk, which all school children were entitled to, and which they usually enjoyed at school. This day was different; they drank it whilst sitting on the platform in the station. Then after enjoying their first school trip they boarded the next train back to Barnsley and school.

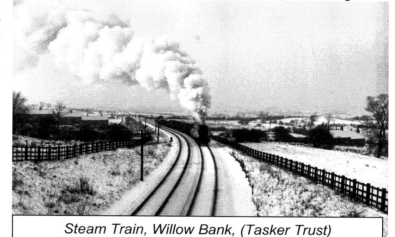

Steam Train, Willow Bank, (Tasker Trust)

A JOURNEY THROUGH HONEYWELL TO RALEY SCHOOL
Don Booker MBE

There were two things prominent on the horizon that could be seen from the classroom at Burton Road Primary School, Old Mill. It was the Town Hall and to the right, the red brick Raley Secondary Modern School.

The only time we looked to the Town Hall was when the tower flag was flying. As for the school, it was the mystery place where the majority would go for the second part of their education. It was a place where boys and girls in those war time years, would walk through the Honeywell district to the segregated school, all because they had failed the Eleven Plus examination.

If you got top marks in the exam, there were places at the Girl's High School or Holgate Grammar School. Then there was the Central School, opposite Holyrood RC Church - known as the jam factory because at one time it was - or Longcar Central, off Racecommon Road.

Raley School, however, had something all the others failed to have - an indoor swimming pool.

My school journey started at 106, Burton Road, Old Mill. I quickly passed the school I had left and was in Eldon Street, with the Star Paper Mill on my right, and then turned down Canal Street along the bank of the canal. This was a short cut through the Honeywell allotments.

Apart from the noise of steam coming from the boilers of the paper mill, there was always another metallic sound from corrugated sheds. We discovered it was the *Nail 'Oyle* where a family business made nails for joiners and builders.

On the other side of the path were the gardens where *Honeywellians* were *'Digging for Victory'* growing their own food. It was also the place where in later years I discovered Reg Mellor, who I introduced to the world of show business - he was the world ferret-legging champion.

Once out of the gardens I headed for Honeywell Lane, but always called at a small grocery shop on the corner. Not for sweets - they were rationed - but for a raw carrot or small turnip.

Under the railway bridge and first left was Raley School, where on our first day we nervously faced another exam to select us for the school streaming. Results meant we either went in A1, B1 or Remove - what a title! But usually those who were in Remove never did move in all their years at the school.

Raley was an exciting place, because in addition to the baths, it had metal and woodwork classrooms, science room and gymnasium, plus a dining room. I was asked to help with the serving of the dinner and my speciality was the big gravy jug.

In my class I had a lovely teacher, Mrs Amy Bambridge, a widow from the First World War. She was a specialist in music, and at the Remembrance Day services in the hall, she would play the piano with tears streaming down her face.

We got on well because I was keen on music and played the trumpet. One of her more unusual requests was to occasionally ask that we scratch her back with a school ruler!

The headmaster was Henry Bird, who at Christmas asked if I would form a band to play at concerts. I did, with an extra perk of playing at concerts also in the girls' school. This brought a special privilege, an invitation to *The Cottage* where the girls were taught domestic duties and was a *'no go'* area for boys. We were served tea - usually Spam sandwiches and jelly and custard.

Raley was an exciting place, because we were taught gardening by Mr. Edson, who was always sun-tanned because he was always in the garden, but also taught maths. We also bred rabbits - in the school boiler house.

After two years, Raley School had totally stimulated my educational ability. I sat examinations for a teacher training school at Longcar Central and also for Barnsley Technical School - passing both and deciding on the latter.

My grandparents, Tom and Elizabeth Booker, lived on Old Bridge Street, where on occasions I would miss a school dinner and visit them. I would walk down that dark stone passage from Old Bridge Street to Honeywell Street, passing the mystery door which I later discovered was a boxing club.

I played with the Symcox, Potter and Goodliffe lads for years, and we at times had a battle with the young *Honeywellians*.

Looking back, Raley School, Old Bridge and Honeywell Streets with their chip and sweet shops, provided me with a foundation for later life. It taught me what friendship was about.

After a struggle, it took me to the height of my profession; to be honoured by Her Majesty the Queen and by my home town. The Queen made me a Member of the Order of the British Empire, and the town made me one of the Millennium Heroes, both for helping the Community of Barnsley and for Services to Journalism.

Today Raley School looks down on the Honeywell district just like Buckingham Palace looks down The Mall.

Don, receiving his MBE (Member of the Order of the British Empire), from 'Her Majesty the Queen'

MEMORIES OF HONEYWELL (Raley or Hollywood!)
Sheila Brown

My family had always lived in isolated country cottages, until following the outbreak of the 1939 War and my father's subsequent departure into the army, when we moved to a small industrial town.

Instead of roaming the fields and woods, gathering lilies of the valley in the hills in spring, playing in the hayfields in summer, picking blackberries and hazel nuts in the autumn, sledging in winter, along with all the activities around animals in this rural background, I was now living in a densely populated area which at first was most intimidating. I was soon instructed in the ways of urban childhood by the many children who lived nearby, especially to the glamorous world of 'the pictures.' This was called Hollywood!

There were two cinemas within a few minutes walk, each showing two programmes every week. Many of the main feature films were classified as 'A' for adult viewing, and others were classified 'U' for universal viewing where children could go alone. Many of the films were 'A' but it was general practice to approach an adult near the cinema entrance, preferably a lone man, hold out the few coins for a ticket and ask "Will you take me in please?" Inevitably, he complied, took the money and got a child's ticket with his own, took you past the usherette at the door of the auditorium and left you free to find a seat alone, preferably as near to the front as possible to get a good view, and join other children who had got inside by the same means.

For a very small price, the entertainment consisted of the main long film, a shorter supporting film, a comedy starring for instance 'The Three Stooges,' whose main activity seemed to centre on hitting each other over the head with a blunt instrument without it resulting in any lasting damage. However, we were never warned against trying such an activity ourselves. Obviously children in this era were assumed to have the necessary common sense and self-discipline, without being told. I never saw any children misbehave, even at a Saturday matinee, when the majority of the patrons were children, particularly if the main picture was a 'U.'

Although 'A' films were considered unsuitable for unaccompanied children to see, the really frightening part of the programme was 'The News' where film of the marching German soldiers invading other countries was shown, and we knew that they intended doing the same here. We had experienced the bombs dropping from the German aircraft. We were well aware that the 'News' was a reality, not Hollywood.

Raley School Swimming Baths – year unknown (courtesy of Barnsley MBC's Archives)

After 1942, I had moved to a rural village near Barnsley and had to travel to Barnsley Girls High School, which I found frightening. One day we were told to bring bathing costumes as we were being taken to Raley. I had no idea where or what Raley was, and was far too shy to ask anyone. My class was marched along Huddersfield Road and then turned off into unknown territory. By this time I had surmised that we were to be taught to swim, which threw me into a panic because when I lived in the Peak District, the only place to swim was the river, where I had been swept away and saved from drowning by the older children when I got caught up in the reeds. So I was scared of running water.

On arrival at Raley, I was amazed to find it was a large very modern school for boys and girls, aged eleven to fourteen. That was the age at which children left school. That place had everything: housecraft, cookery, workshops, and even a heated indoor swimming pool. So this was Raley, a school with a swimming bath, but to me it was like things I had seen at the cinema, Hollywood!

MEMORIES OF RALEY SCHOOL – MUM AND DAUGHTER
Julie Johnson (nee Fieldsend)

My mum, Lillian Fieldsend (nee Copley), was born at John Edward Street off Honeywell Street in 1922. At some point the family also lived nearby in Sarah Ann Street. Having moved to Smithies at some time before the age of eleven, she was one of the first intake of pupils at the newly opened Raley School, Honeywell Lane, in 1933.

Like mum, I too attended Raley School at the age of eleven, back in 1967, when Secondary Modern was attached to the name. Living on Doncaster Road, the school fell within the catchment area of my home. The walk from home through the town and up onto Huddersfield Road, where the top entrance (Cockerham Lane) was, felt like quite a distance after my previous two-minute walk to Doncaster Road Infant/Junior School. This took about forty-five minutes plus another five minutes down the long path to the school site. Alternatively I could walk through town, down Eldon Street, along Honeywell Street and up Honeywell Lane to the other school entrance, known as the bottom way.

Like many children thought, on first appearance, the size of the school was quite daunting compared to my previous school, but the many facilities provided by the school soon made up for it. A large separate block at the back of the school housed a gym and swimming pool (left-hand side). On the right-hand side there were woodwork and metalwork classrooms with appropriate fixtures and fittings – but I never went inside that part of the block as girls just didn't have the opportunity to learn those subjects in those days.

The main school building had two floors with an internal quadrangle – I suppose for sitting outside, but I don't remember this ever being used. The ground floor had separate entrances, the left-hand side for girls and right-hand side for boys. Only staff and visitors to the school used the main central entrance. The ground floor had (from the left side moving towards the central area) toilets, opposite the entrance, and cloakrooms (rows of pegs and sinks with mirrors above), music room, staff room and rooms to hold caretaking/servicing equipment and supplies.

Upstairs all the classrooms including sewing, cooking, headmaster's and secretary's office followed the quadrangle shape. At either side of the central staircase upstairs were two halls with a stage and access to a small library. The halls were used not only for morning assembly but also for other activities like rehearsing for plays or dancing. The cooking or domestic science rooms (two) had storage rooms for ingredients and baking equipment. Between the two cookery rooms was a two-storey flat where girls could learn and practice home management skills.

In sporting terms, the field adjacent to the front of the main building accommodated the playing of hockey, rounders and running on sports days. A netball/tennis court was on a lower level at the bottom right-hand side of the drive to Honeywell Lane. Across the road from the bottom of this drive was a very large field where athletics, field events, football and cricket took place. Opportunities to flourish in any sporting events were available to those with talent. Every child adopted a house name and you joined others with the same house name when competing in sporting activities. These names were planet themed – Mars, Saturn, Jupiter and Venus. I was in Saturn house, and we always seemed to do fairly well at sports.

The refectory or canteen, as it was more commonly known, was an antiquated separate building at the top of Honeywell Lane drive, opposite the sports field. It looked like an air raid shelter with a corrugated iron roof but much bigger. Basic, but functional. Large tables ran up either side in rows with a central walkway to the serving counter and kitchen behind. I think it seated eight pupils (four on either side of each table); two of the pupils were given the task of servers of the meal, serving from containers, probably for a term, then someone else would be designated the task. Metal jugs of water were provided and plastic beakers for drinking. Metal jugs were also used for serving custard. The whole thing had a regimented feel to it and *messing about* wasn't tolerated.

For the last two years I took sandwiches and ate them at a friend's house in Old Mill Lane near to the school. In her bedroom, we would read the 'Jackie' magazine and drool at the double-spread size posters which had been removed, and put on her bedroom wall. David Cassidy of 'The Partridge Family' was a particular favourite of hers. On Fridays, as a treat, we would have fish cake and chips from Pearson's Fish and Chip shop in Old Mill Lane which was then opposite the Prince of Wales pub. Gorgeous fish and chips!!

From 1968/69, Mr. Chambers was the Head teacher, but was replaced by Mr. Alwyn Jones from 1969/72. He was a fairly quiet unassuming man, but firm and fair when he had to be. Deputy Head teacher was Mrs Garbutt who was very strict, especially when it came to things like girls wearing too short a skirt, make-up and jewellery. She had a strong Welsh accent, and wore glasses rather like 'Dame Edna' as I recall - a real character!

Going home via the Honeywell Lane exit you had to go under the railway bridge, affectionately locally known as the "monkey tunnel." Along Honeywell Street, walking towards Old Mill Lane there was a row of terraced houses and outside one of them hung a cage with a Mynah bird inside. As you passed it would talk and mimic sounds and words if you called to it. Children would often call to it to try and get it to talk. That row of houses is no longer there, having been replaced by council flats. On one particular occasion I remember walking on Honeywell Street, when I noticed someone washing and polishing a red VW Beetle car. I immediately recognised him as Brian Glover, who had become famous as the brash P.E. teacher from the film 'Kes.' I smiled at him, but didn't dare speak to him as I was rather shy.

In June 1984, I moved to Honeywell with my husband and two boys, not long after the beginning of the Miners' Strike. In 1987, I began working at Honeywell School (the school's name had changed from Raley to Honeywell in 1973) as a lunchtime supervisory assistant – in other words a "dinner lady." I didn't expect it at the time, but this was to be the last year Honeywell would be used as a school, as it was to be taken over as part of the Barnsley College Campus network. Since I had been a pupil at the school, some changes had been made in terms of modifications to the building, especially with the addition of a school dining room, which had been built onto the main school building. This gave a more contemporary and welcoming look and feel to lunchtimes. The old refectory had become obsolete.

The school was due to close in July 1988 and many pupils and children were sad and unhappy about it. It was the end of an era. To commemorate the school, a plate and mug was commissioned, and Mr. Clancy the art teacher designed the artwork. Staff at the school were able to buy a set of the limited edition plate and mug, so I purchased a set, and bought one for Mum too, to mark the occasion as one of the first intake of pupils. These I will keep as fond memories of the school, where mum and daughter had attended the school at the beginning and at the end. I bet many people can't say that!

Mr Alwyn Jones (Headmaster), presenting a trophy to a runner (circa 1971) (Barnsley Archives)

Commemorative Cup and Plate

MY LIFE AT RALEY SCHOOL (1955)
Maurice Cawthorne

In 1954 my family moved house, from Barnsley into a new housing estate called Athersley North. I was aged ten years and attended Athersley Junior School until I was eleven years old. The new school I was to attend after the eleven plus exam was Edward Sheerian, but at that time, in 1955, it was still in the process of being built, therefore I had to attend Raley School, which was situated just off Honeywell Lane in Barnsley.

The headmaster was Mr. Parkinson and the school was split in two, boys being on one side, girls on the other.

My time at Raley was a bit complicated because only the first half of the week was spent there; for the second half, I had to go to Wilthorpe School. To get to Raley I would travel by bus to town. I remember walking along Honeywell Street each day, where there was a large cage hanging outside one of the houses. In it was a 'Mynah Bird' and every time I passed, it would squawk loudly, "Hello Maurice." To this day I wonder who told it my name, ha ha! (Only kidding), but it did give me a loud *wolf-whistle* every time I passed by.

The second half of my school week was spent at Wilthorpe, where Mr. Griffiths was headmaster. On the day of the changeover from Raley to Wilthorpe, we did a 'cross country' run via the area known as Willow Bank.

Raley School was quite special really, because it boasted its own swimming pool. I think it was probably the only one in the area because pupils were brought in to use it from schools all around the borough;

Raley School, Canteen (Barnsley Archive)

it was situated at the back of the school. The dining room was a separate building on the right-hand side of the school.

FIFTIETH ANNIVERSARY OF RALEY/HONEYWELL SCHOOL (1983)
(Taken from the Commemorative Booklet produced at the time, provided by Katherine Symcox)
Julie Johnson

Raley school owes its existence to the Hadow Report of 1927, which advocated a separate system of secondary education for all pupils from the age of eleven. In March 1930, eleven-and-a-half acres of land was purchased adjoining Honeywell Lane, at a cost of £1,750 and architects, Dyson, Cawthorne and Coles were engaged to design the proposed school.

The site had to be levelled, and familiar local red brick dressed with Huddersfield stone, was used to build the school and topped with grey and green slates. The final cost of the building was £35,157 and £2,234 was spent on equipment. It was introduced as a Senior Elementary School and was intended for those children who did not qualify for admission to Grammar, Technical or Central Schools. Initially it was proposed that the school be given its present name "Honeywell School," but was eventually decided that it be called "Raley School," after the Chairman of the Education Committee.

The school opened in 1933, with a special emphasis on the fact that a "Wireless Installation" and a Swimming Pool (referred to as "The Plunge" by Mr. Bird), would be available for use by the pupils.

The school was divided into a Girls' Department under Miss Chambers and a Boys' Department under Mr. Bird. Facilities for boys and girls were the same, apart from the Craft curriculum, which reflected the traditional division between the sexes, boys doing wood, metal work and gardening and girls doing cookery, laundry, housewifery, pottery and weaving. For the girls, emphasis was also on 'Fine Art' in all its forms, making the Girls Department more "progressive." Boys had shown particular appreciation of the gymnasium and swimming baths. The gardens and greenhouse to the rear of Belle Vue House were available for the use of the school.

Innovative features were school camps e.g. at Scout Dike, and the introduction of Wireless Broadcasts as part of the curriculum.

Regular features were Parent/Open Days, Medical/Dental Inspections, annual School Concerts, Swimming/Life Saving classes and Royal Life Saving Awards (Bronze) and other awards.

Conclusion

At its beginning, the Education Committee had erected not only a well equipped, but a beautiful school in quiet, pleasant surroundings which will have had no small influence in the refinement of character.

On its Fiftieth Anniversary, the best tribute of all perhaps to Raley School, was the fact that many of the aims and much of the basic content of the curriculum remained the same for Honeywell School some 50 years later.

CLOSURE OF HONEYWELL SCHOOL (1988)
Mark Steele

I attended Honeywell Secondary School, formerly Raley, between 1983 and 1988. My first week was spent walking round in a daze, bumping into people and getting lost, but I eventually got used to it. My form teacher was Mr. Blenkinsopp, and his class was just across from the library.

The headmaster of the school was Mr. Alwyn Jones. My classmates included: Swerdy, Speedy, Foggy, Thunder, Boo and Oggy. In my opinion some of the teachers were overly strict, but most were ok. If you were targeted by a school bully at break-time, then you might get bundled down a little stairwell, (the Gozpit) and *gozzed* on, but luckily I managed to avoid that gruesome experience.

My greatest sporting achievement was scoring a try, one muddy yet memorable games period. Unfortunately I couldn't manage to convert it – kicking the ball hopefully, then watching it *scoot* feebly across the bumpy turf between the posts; what an embarrassment!

One day all the kids decided to take after the miners and go out on strike. We rampaged across the fields after lunchtime bawling "strike, strike, strike!" and refusing to return for afternoon lessons. Gradually, we came to our senses and scurried back inside, leaving just a few hardened strikers or troublemakers out there. Even they had to face the music in the end and bow to the inevitable!

During my final year, I was aware of the plans to close Honeywell and make it part of Barnsley College. Lots of people protested but no-one really seemed to take much notice. I was busy getting through my last few months of coursework and exams, so I could leave the place.

The following autumn, I started at college only to find myself sitting back in my old school classroom again. It seemed I couldn't escape!

Footnote: *Mark has included a photograph, taken by Sheffield Star newspaper of all the school children fighting for the cause, see page 74.*

Raley Girls' Modern School Choir broadcasting from Leeds on January 10 1950, with Miss Chambers conducting.
(S)

*School children taken around the time of the
closure of Honeywell School in 1988.
(Courtesy of Sheffield Star newspaper).*

Beckett Street School c 1929-1, Dorothy Frost.

Eldon Street School, 1933- 35

5A, Eldon Street School 51/52

Tom Outwin, Becket Street School 1930

Eldon Street School, Betty Hollingsworth, forth right front row

Eldon Street School 1954, Elaine Miller

Eldon Street School 1954, Gloria Phillips, second right second row

Eldon Street School 1962, Maxine Glover, first row third from left

Eldon Street School 1953-54, Mary Phillips, first left second row, Elaine Fidler, third left second row

ELDON STREET
Junior Mixed School
BARNSLEY. 1952.

BARNSLEY HIGH SCHOOL FOR GIRLS
Sue Fallis (was Hutson)

A front entrance so grand
Only teachers could use
Long dreary corridors
Black lace-up shoes
Two ounces of Midget Gems
To cure afternoon blues
A uniform definitely designed not to flatter
If you bothered to moan, it never did matter;
Drab grey it was, with a tie of plain red
With a beret worn sensibly upon one's head.

But the life skills they taught
Were a lot less fraught.
Fine manners were an essential part
And impressed others from the start.

"Don't cause folk to step into the road"
No more than two abreast, was our 'pavement code'
"Don't leave any litter in the school grounds,"
If you do, then the 'litter code' abounds.
All the school was made to pay
By losing our half-day holiday.
Giving up to an adult, your bus seat
Was considered to be kind and sweet;
Our reserved behaviour in the street
Kept our good reputation complete.

One last idea springs to my mind
As we from 'ladettes to ladies' became;
That those regulation grey knickers we wore
Should be placed in the school's "Hall of Fame!"

GOING OFF TO GRAMMAR SCHOOL
Marion McManis (nee Smith)

It's 1955, and off to join the heady ranks of Barnsley Girls' High School. This was approximately ten years after the end of World War 2.

Money was scarce; the uniform list endless, and it had to be worn accurately to the last button. Thankfully, there were uniform grants which helped towards its purchase. These had to be spent at prescribed shops such as Butterfields and Massies.

sixpence per day, but free for the less well off. I knew that I was one of the "less well off," when I queued to collect my first weekly dinner tickets. Mine were white with "FREE DINNER" proclaimed in large block capital letters across the front. The "two and sixers" had pink tickets, which clearly displayed the price paid.

The dinner tickets had to be handed over every dinner-time to the prefect in charge of your table, and always in full view of your peers. Embarrassing to be sure, but I don't remember it ever spoiling my appetite!

High School 1960, Marion McManis, back row second left

High School, year unknown

High School 1962, Elaine Fidler first row first left

High School 1971, Maxine Glover, back row second left

Raley School 1936.

Raley School 1936, Doris Gosling, back row second right

Raley School Staff, 1953-1954

Raley School, 'Gypsy Dance' Brenda Marsden (Frost)

Raley School, Prefects 1960

'Easy Money' by pupils of Raley School

84

My Life
Bill Westwood

I retain memories of a wonderful early life on Honeywell Street (No 82), from 1940 when I was born, to 1962 when I married and moved to Granville Street. There were lots of great people in Honeywell, and the one common denominator was that virtually everyone had very little money. The only car on the street belonged to Fred Barry and he garaged it on his allotment so he didn't have the parking problems that there are today. Because people had little money, they also didn't have possessions that other people may have wanted, so there were no break-ins or stealing.

Everybody tended to look after their neighbours, if they were ill or not; I remember my mother looked after one neighbour for years. As kids, you just walked into the houses of one of your playmates without ever knocking and vice versa. To put that into context, I have never even been in another house on the street where I now live, and I have lived on the street for nineteen years.

My earliest memory is of going to Wilthorpe Infants School, as a two year old because my mother worked there and there was no one to look after me otherwise. I then graduated to Beckett Street Infants School when I was three in 1943, and my main memory of that was of the cots in the hall where everyone had to sleep in the afternoon. This was the period before the NHS was introduced and there were loads of illnesses that occurred, with limited access to a doctor, and I suffered badly from ear, nose and throat (ENT) problems, and ultimately I had to have my tonsils out. I can remember waking up after the operation and being given a sweet, which I thought was marvellous until I found out that my mother had brought me the sweets (which were under rationing) and all the other kids in the ward had been given one of my sweets.

My dad worked down the pit all his life, a lot of the time on the coalface and had been as strong as an ox. Ultimately though, like a lot of other miners, he developed asthma, bronchitis and emphysema and had to leave the face and got a button job with a vast reduction in pay. Even with this job there were long periods when he could not work, and as a result, my mother had to work full time to keep the house running. Given these circumstances, I never wanted for anything, for which I was eternally grateful to them (even if I did not always show it).

During the winter of 1947 the snow was three foot deep. The toilet was across the yard and I can remember the path in the snow to the toilet, and the snow level being above my head. It was like that for two months through February and March. Later, when the snow had melted, my mother would take my trousers off (no pants) and send me across the yard to the toilet. At that time, Fred Berry had some hens and two cockerels which he kept in a hen house in the yard. These cockerels, which were big, used to hate me and would chase me, and once chased me through the ginnel into Honeywell Street. The bus stop was just outside our house and there were a number of people waiting (and laughing) when I ran to the front door with no trousers on with the cockerels after me. I took revenge on them later when I pushed the hen house over.

When I was young, I had no fear of heights or anything, and my dad said that when they wanted me, they looked up a tree. Twice I was involved in incidents where I could have been killed. The first time was when I fell off the wall, at the bottom of Honeywell Street. The second time was when I climbed into a trailer, behind a car, in Honeywell Lane and jumped out as it was being driven along Honeywell Street. Both times I landed on my head, and suffered concussion and kept in hospital for twenty-four hours. Once I was playing with a friend, in the Willow Bank and he had an air pistol. I knew that he did not have any pellets so that when he told me to put my hand over the end of the barrel to feel the percussion, I did so not knowing he had put an elderberry into the pistol. He found it very funny that it raised a large blood blister on my hand.

In the late forties we used to spend most of the summer months in the Willow Bank, playing and just returned home when we were hungry. There was no problem with water as there was a spring by the canal which gave the coldest cleanest water I have ever drunk. At that time, the chimney over the air shaft at the abandoned colliery was still standing, and somehow we managed to make a hole in the chimney and dropped stones down the shaft, which was about two hundred feet deep. Again, we had no concept of danger and were only stopped when the NCB demolished the chimney and capped the shaft. These cappings are there to this day.

To alleviate hunger, we used to go to Bruno's Raspberry Plantation, which is now Hall Balk Estate. We either picked the raspberries officially and were paid 4d (2p) a punnet which was 1lb of raspberries, and also ate as much as we wanted, or we would cross over the railway line by Tinkers Pond and then eat as much as we liked unofficially. When we were coming home we would call in the orchards on Cockerham Lane for apples and pears, or strawberries on Carrington Avenue.

Late August or early September we would be collecting conkers even though they were not ready, and hours would be spent either climbing the trees or throwing sticks to knock them off. In early September we started collecting *bunny wood*, chopping branches off the trees and storing the logs in the air raid shelters. Between collecting, we would guard the logs all evening, even though everyone else would be guarding their logs, so no-one was likely to steal them anyway. On bonfire night, the fire was held in the middle of Honeywell Street between John Edward Street and Sarah Ann Street and was a magnificent affair. Buses could not get past and had to go down John Edward Street and up Sarah Ann Street and vice versa, and the council had to repair the road afterwards.

A lad we knew had been selling canes to us for bows and arrows and we found out where he was getting them from – it was a house on Honeywell Grove - so we cut out the middle man and began to take them ourselves. Unfortunately there were so many of us stealing them that we were noticed and were reported to the police. There were more than twenty children who had to go to the police station to be given a severe warning.

Regarding entertainment, there were no televisions, although we did have a radio in our house. As a result we entertained ourselves. During the winter we played football until it was dark and then *allevio*. The den was in front of Gunhouses' shop, until we were called in for bed. The football matches took place in the yard behind Fred Sharp's house and the goals were the toilet entrances at the top and the bottom of the yard. We never had a proper football and used tennis balls of which we had a plentiful supply. We used to collect the rejects (unofficially) from Slazengers plant at Measboro' Dike. There was just one problem with this venue - it was Ernest Ward, the rag and bone man who lived by the centre circle. He had a habit of chasing us out of the yard. He kept his cart in the yard, and after he had chased us out of the yard, we would go back and start swinging on the arms of the cart, pulling the cart down. He would then chase us again and say, "I wish I could get my hands on you," and we would say, "you'll have to wish in one hand and s.... in the other," which made him even happier.

Sunken Barge Canal and Keel Inn, (Tasker Trust)

During the summer it was always cricket, this time played in our back yard. We could not play football because there was a nine inch step halfway across the yard. The stumps were a dustbin, the bat a piece of wood sawn to shape and the usual tennis balls.

We also went fishing in the canal, either by the Keel Inn or in the Willow Bank; in both places there were sunken barges in which fish collected. They were also dangerous because at that time the canal was six feet deep and the sides of the barges were thin and you could have easily fallen into the water, which I managed to do once and someone had to pull me out.

It was a fact that in those early days you were not taught to swim. The first time I went to a swimming baths was when I was in the fourth year at Eldon Street Juniors and the class was taken for lessons at Raley Baths.

Beano and progressing to the Rover Adventure Wizard and Hotspur, which I read every week. I also visited the public library junior section and I read almost every volume in the boys section. I also spent many a happy hour in the museum there.

Further entertainment was on Sunday mornings with the pigeon racers in the Keel Field. These birds were milers and with a following wind could fly the mile in less than sixty seconds. The race used to start from a different starting point every week, each one a mile from the Keel Field, and during the week they would practice from that week's particular starting point, and then on Sunday the race would take place. More than twenty birds took part and the winning bird's owner took the cash prize from the one pound entrance fee whilst the spectators gambled on the result. When the race finished everyone went into the Keel Inn which was always full. Then afterwards at closing time, a number would play football in Docks (Dockerty's) field and we would join in, this time with a proper football.

Another speciality was Chuck Brownley's boxing gym which was in the yard behind the Honeywell Inn. We used to go in the gym and watch the grown-ups boxing, and then afterwards we were allowed to use the punch bag, and punch ball and skipping ropes, and also to put on the 16oz gloves and box in the ring.

At other times we would go into Symcox's stable which was in the yard at the back of Colin Bowran's house and spend hours making bundles of firewood which they used to sell. They had metal rings, three inches in diameter and two inches high, and we would stack sticks into the rings and then wrap a piece of wire around the sticks to hold them. We were never paid for all the work and just did it for the enjoyment.

I used to play with Arnold Midgeley a lot, and spent a lot of time in his house which was the end house, before the Garden House. I normally sat near the window, but on this particular day I was sitting at the other side of the room, when a lorry that had been left with the brakes off ran down the street, and crashed into the house, and left a heap of rubble where I normally sat. We used to jump across the garden path, from the wall at the back of Arnolds house, across the roof of the Garden House. This gap was about four feet, and there was a drop of about sixteen feet between them. The Garden House was the oldest house on the street, and was probably built around the sixteenth century. The toilet was a *midden*, which had to be emptied at intervals by the council, which wasn't a very pleasant job, especially so when someone threw a coconut matting into it.

Home coal deliveries happened virtually every day because most of the people in the area worked at the pits. I used to get the coal in from being aged seven years onwards. We used to make sure that people like Mrs White had enough coal and sold some of the deliveries when our cellar was full. Mrs Taylor used to bake her own bread and she used to place the oven bottom cakes on the back window sill to cool down. I can still remember the smell of the freshly-baked bread to this day; it was even better than the smell in Asda when they are baking their bread.

We used to play marbles on the small patch of ground in front of the houses from Booth's to Danforth's. We always had a plentiful supply of marbles from Redfearns, unofficially. There used to be a large shed at Redfearns where they used to store sacks and this was *mecca* for us because we could jump about on the sacks exactly like on a hay bale. Unfortunately, the sacks were filthy and we used to return home as black as the ace of spades!

The picture houses were the biggest source of entertainment in those days and we always went to the Ritz on Saturday mornings to see the "Three Stooges" and "Abbott & Costello" films. I once remember queuing for an hour in the rain at the Alhambra to see "High Noon." At that time in the early fifties, cinemas were not allowed to open on Sundays, so they showed films at Raley School on Sunday night which were very well attended. When cinemas were allowed to open on Sundays we had to queue completely round the block at the Ritz which was always filled.

Another memory was of the "set pot" in the kitchen which was always in use. Mondays it was washing day and I recall building my muscles up using the cast iron mangle and the Peggy tub. Then the rest of the week it was used for meals: stew meat, ham shanks and pig hocks, and the occasional piece of horsemeat obtained from the knackers yard in Twibell Street. Speaking of that, I can still recall the stench created when they were boiling and the wind was from the east.

I slept with my mother and dad in their bedroom until I was eighteen, and it was great when my sister married and I moved into a room of my own. I don't know how people with large families managed.

Another memory is of Chuck Philips and one of the Bickertons having a fist fight; no kicking in those days. It took place in the middle of Honeywell Street in front of Mrs Bickerton's house, in the middle of a ring formed by about two hundred people, so it was well advertised, and it went on for ages.

During the school holidays we used to go to the Public Hall for lunch; this was a three-course meal for 10d (4p). They used to cater for 600 people at a time. The tables were in the concert hall and the meals were served on the stage.

Another feature was the Mynah bird that belonged to Mrs Bickerton. This was held in a cage which was on the wall in front of their house. It spoke exactly like Mrs Bick, it used to attract the attention of everyone who went past.

In the late forties Colin Bowran's father had a gramophone player, the only one that I knew of in the area. It was one of the original HMV models with the elongated horn. It played the old 12" shellac records, using the exchangeable needles which they didn't have many of, so the needles were blunt and the records scratched, but we still thought the whole system was amazing. Again in the late forties the Honeywell pub was the focus of entertainment and was always busy, afternoon and night. We spent many hours on the windowsill in the summer evenings, listening to the people singing to the piano.

Another memory is of Mabel Pickersgill's beer-off shop in Old Mill Lane. She had an order every day for beer for the workers at the Paper Mill and especially Redfearns; she used to sell nearly as much beer as the pubs. What was amazing was the number of fish and chip shops that there were in the area: two in Eldon St. North, two in Old Mill Lane and one on Honeywell Street, all very good shops doing good business selling chips at 2d (1p) and fish at 5d (21/2p). Taking the focal point of the junction of Honeywell Street and Old Mill Lane, it was no more than 100 yards to any of the shops.

Another shop doing very good business was the pop and sweet shop across from Eldon Street School. He sold 1d glasses of pop from quart bottles to most of the children at the school. I also remember the excellent ice cream from Palfreyman's, either from the factory which was between Eldon St. North and Old Mill Lane, or from his delivery van that Keith or his father drove round. Further memories are of Len who went around the area on Saturday night calling out 'Green un' and Ras Prince Monolulu the tipster, shouting, "I gotta horse" for anyone prepared or daft enough to pay for the tips. Then there was the horse and cart from the Co-op Dairy delivering milk.

I had many happy times at Eldon St. Juniors and always stayed for the school meals which were 4d (2p) a day. In my last year at the school the King & Queen were due to visit Barnsley, and one of the things Barnsley Council organised was a mass choir of the children from the fourth forms of all the junior schools in the town. Although I didn't make the choir, my mother took me to the Town Hall to watch, and I sang anyway. Later that term, the school presented Widecombe Fair at the Alhambra Theatre, and I played Uncle Tom Cobley. I think the only reason why I got the part was because they had obtained a Mobo horse for Tom, and I was the only one small enough to ride it. Just before the school closed for the summer, a trip had been organised to the Festival of Britain in London, and that was the first time in my life that I had been out of Barnsley.

I took the Eleven Plus exam during the summer, and waited after the school closed for the results of the exam. I was in bed one morning, when Chris Rounds ran up the stairs and said, "You have passed to go to the grammar school." I said to him, "How do you know," and he said "I guessed". He had in fact opened my letter. This opened a life for me, as only five pupils from Eldon Street School had passed the Eleven Plus exam, two boys and three girls. The other boy, David Green, was a teacher's son, and was extremely gifted and went immediately into the 'A' stream at Holgate. I was in the 'B' stream, which was quite an achievement as there were five streams. I made quite a few friends at the school, and as a result of the after school activities and the homework, I drifted away from my friends of the Eldon Street era, although I continued my friendship with John Taylor, who I still see to this day.

We started going to the YMCA in the evenings and at weekends. I took the G.C.E. exams in 1956 and obtained six passes at 'O' level. I took the final exam on Monday, went to Woodmoor Pit, 4 and 5 on Tuesday, saw Jack Sykes, the Under manager, and was given a job and started on Wednesday afternoon at 2 p.m. until 10 p.m.; what an eye opener. The job was on the surface, pulling muck tubs out of the tipper (which was worked by Bill Philips from Honeywell Street), and pushing the tubs to a hoist, and back down the pit. I was never unemployed again until I retired. I did my underground training; eight weeks at Woolley and eight weeks at Barnsley Tech., then worked underground in the safety staff from January. I was put in charge of six other staff members, and was responsible for the air flow measurement, and for the collection of air and dust samples taken by the staff.

During this time, I entered an essay competition, with six others from other European nations, organised by the E.E.C., for which the first prize was a trip to Europe. I won the competition, and travelled down to Heathrow to fly to Brussels. It was March, 1958 and there had been the Manchester United air crash in February. The plane I flew in was an Elizabethan, just like the Manchester United one. I was seventeen years old and had never flown before, and was unaccompanied by anyone. The all-expenses paid trip involved visits to Brussels, The Hague, Arnhem, Cologne and Dusseldorf, and was a fantastic experience.

I continued to study at the college, and at twenty-three years old, obtained a First Class Colliery Managers Certificate and an H.H.D. in Mining. Chris Rounds had also obtained his Managers Certificate. It is an achievement in itself to obtain this certificate, and for two next door neighbours, given our circumstances, was truly amazing. Chris quickly obtained an Under Managers post and within a short time a Manager's post, followed by an Agent's post which involved two Collieries; a staggering achievement.

The pits didn't work out for me, because I began suffering from asthma in 1963. I began looking for another job and had a fantastic stroke of luck. I met an old colleague from the Tech., who I had not seen for years, and he told me he was working for the N.C.B. Computer Services at Doncaster and that they were always looking for staff. I applied, and to cut a long story short was appointed as a Computer Programmer in January 1966. I had twenty-seven wonderful years in a job that I always enjoyed, and to make things even better, my asthma disappeared four months after being out of the pit.

As I mentioned before, I left the street in 1962, but I never left its principles and I always treat people how I would like them to treat me.

'Us' or 'we' includes any, or all of: John Taylor, Ray Brown, Joe Land, Peter Christon, Melvin Charlesworth, Chris Rounds, Ronny Smith, Doug Lovitt, Cyril Berry, Colin Bowran, Fred Sharp, Herbert Savage and Terry Mellor.

LOCAL CHURCHES
Brenda Limbert

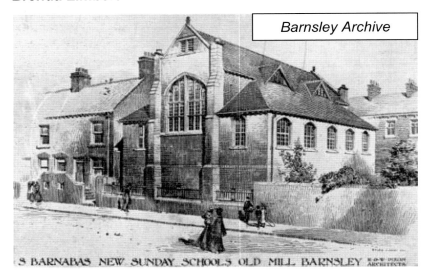

Barnsley Archive

S BARNABAS NEW SUNDAY SCHOOLS OLD MILL BARNSLEY

Bridge Street Chapel was built in 1888 at the end of Bridge Street, to the left of Bridge Gardens. It was demolished in 1980, and flats now occupy the site.

I remember when Sunday School was at 2.30 p.m. It included a kindergarten class and was held in the vestry where the children were told simplified Bible stories, and drew and coloured their own pictures to illustrate the stories. The older children were allowed in the main building and would take part in singing hymns etc. Half-way through, the service would split into smaller classes where they were also told Bible stories and encouraged to draw pictures. Older children were able to participate in learning set passages from the Bible, for which they were awarded a special Bible each, this was a custom established in accordance with the will of Philip Lord Wharton who died in 1696. I personally received mine when I was fifteen years of age.

The 6 p.m. Evensong was held specifically for adults and older children. Holy Communion was taken at this service, often with lay preachers in attendance.

Mr. and Mrs Cusworth, who ran a fruit and vegetable business in Eldon Street North, were the superintendents at the chapel at the time I attended, which was from around 1938, and were still superintendents in 1955 when I went less frequently due to becoming a Sunday cyclist. Mrs Stella Masterton was also a regular figure at the chapel, and played the piano for services when Mr. Egan, who was the organist, wasn't able to be there.

Mrs Masterton also took the kindergarten class, and among the many tasks she took part in was the annual visit to Gomersall, near Leeds, which was very popular with a lot of the children. We travelled by public transport to one of Mrs Masterson's relatives who kept a farm there. We were treated to rides on a pony and trap, and afterwards played games and picnicked in the fields. The weather seemed to warrant outside picnics in those days.

Another popular figure at the chapel was a Mr. Topham, who took a class of boys in the vestry, where they did similar things to the girls' classes - Bible stories etc.

The annual prize-giving day was usually held on a Sunday afternoon, and books were awarded for good attendance. There was also Anniversary Sunday, another annual event, when we held a concert, which was avidly looked forward to and always well received. Of course there was also the Christmas party with the arrival of Father Christmas to give each child a present. This was always a resounding success.

I also remember St Barnabas Church on Old Mill Lane (one side of the church was on Honeywell Street). The church hasn't been used for religious services for many years now, but is used for Masonic meetings.

Of course there is also St Mary's on Sadler Gate and Church Lane. The foundations of St Mary's date back to the eighth century and the tower to the Norman times. The church was badly damaged by fire and was rebuilt, with the exception of the tower, in 1822.

CRICKET
Allan Williamson

Farmer Wright's field was our Headingley. There'd be three or four of us kicking our heels, but after about half-an-hour there would be enough kids to have a game of cricket. Our stump was a large thin stone balanced upright. The length of the pitch was twenty-two strides to the other end and a brick placed to mark the bowling crease. We always played in the same area whether it was cricket or football, so that grassed area was always short. All around the three sides, the grass was knee high, so that became the boundary of the pitch.

We only had one bat and one ball. It was a toss-up who would be Len Hutton and the only batsman in. The bowler would then pitch. The batter would run to the brick and a run would be scored. As soon as the bowler received the ball, the batsman would stroll back to the wicket end. Sometimes the ball would be slogged into the long grass, and depending on the length of time it took to find it, four or six runs could be earned. Sometimes a lost ball could hold the game up for ages.

We played with a full sized bat and a proper *corky*, the leather practically coming off the ball. We were about ten to thirteen years of age. The lad who owned the bat was called Tony. He was always the first to bat. Once he was '*out for a duck*', and cried out "Ah weren't art anyway, am going hoam, and tecking me bat". Off he went. The next thing his dad came striding down the field and said, "What's this? You've sent our Tony home and not let him *lake*". It was explained that Tony had been bowled out, wouldn't accept it and left on his own accord. Much to our delight, his dad gave him a *right* telling off about sportsmanship and playing fair. He still tried it on in future games, but was threatened with a smack if he did. So much for sportsmanship either way.

Local Lads names not known.

PLAYING OUT
Allan Williamson

It was very rare we played in our own back gardens. Our many adventures took place down the *Lowlands* which was a wild area stretching from the canal bridge in Smithies Lane (now the Fleets), right through to the New Lodge estate. We also played in Farmer Wright's field.

We'd *lake* football and cricket until we were shouted in. Anyone's coat was used to mark out the goal posts and the teams were on an ad-hoc basis. *"Can ah lake?" "Arr but go on their side".* The football was a proper leather one with a rubber bladder that had to be blown up with a bike pump; when hard or soft enough it was laced up.

Often we played in pumps or our only pair of school shoes, unless we had proper football boots, sometimes bought as Christmas or birthday presents. The boots were made of leather, had a toughened leather toe cap, and after cleaning them, dubbin was rubbed in. Football studs were nailed into the soles; woe betide if you lost a stud and had to hobble round the field with three nails digging into your foot, which had worked their way through the sole. Shin pads were made from rolled up newspaper and tucked down whatever socks you were wearing at the time. There were no special shirts then; you played in your school jersey - if you had one.

Our imagination took us playing for Preston North End or Accrington Stanley, for the FA cup at Wembley. We were great because occasionally Waffer Hyde was our coach.

STICKS OR PEGS
Dee Williamson

Like most children, after school, our time was spent in the open air, winter or summer, whatever the weather, *playing out.* It only needed a knock on the door and, on opening it, someone saying, "*A tha laking art*?"

Kids from John Edward Street used to congregate around the street lamps. There was one at the corners of both top and bottom of the street. The one mostly used was outside Mrs Barton's house. We were like moths attracted to a glowing light. Sometimes there could be around twelve kids making a racket.

My favourite game was *sticks*. Two teams were elected, the older lads being the leaders and choosing by fair means or foul who they wanted on their team. Three clothes pegs and a soft ball was all the equipment needed. Two of the wooden pegs were placed upright, slightly apart and leaning on Mrs Barton's outside wall. The third peg resting on top of the leaning two, like a bail in cricket. One team would be throwers, the other, fielders. From a specified distance the throwing member would pitch the ball at the pegs to disperse them and knock the bail off. If he missed he was relegated to the back of the queue of throwers. If the ball bounced off the ground, hit the wall and was caught by the fielders, you were classed as out and went to a designated area called *the den* further along the wall.

Success in knocking down the sticks was greeted with cheers or boos and then the fun began. All the throwers scattered, with the fielders chasing after them. It was up to the fielders, using the ball, to hit the throwers before one of them had a chance to re-erect the sticks. The tactics would be to entice a fielder to throw the ball; if the ball was dodged the target would try to erect the sticks and gain a point for his/her team. If you were hit by the ball you were classed as out and sent to the den. The aim of the fielders was to *get out* all the throwers before the sticks could be set up, and a point awarded to the fielders. Many a time someone would be frantically erecting the sticks, and while doing so would receive a thwack of the ball on their back - disappointingly out. Then a triumphant cry of "Sticks!" amid cheers of delight from other throwers. A set number of games were played, then fielders became throwers and vice versa.

If you were out early, most of the time was spent in the den, and you'd cheer your team on, perform handstands, thump the wall with one leg, or sing. All these activities took part on the outside of Mrs. Barton's living room wall. Of course she would tolerate us for so long, and then ask us to move on. How she put up with us night after night – she must have had the patience of a saint. We respected her wishes and moved on to the lamp at the bottom of the street to continue our game.

'Pleasant View' Football team '1947'

'Honeywell Ladies' Football Team 1926-27

'Raley School Cricket' (Barnsley Archive)

PIGEON RACING
Allan Williamson

Pigeon racing was a popular sport amongst the mining communities in Barnsley, be it long distance or pigeons that just flew very fast over a mile, hence *milers*. In the 1950's a meeting took place to look at the feasibility of forming a miler pigeon club in the Honeywell area. What followed was an agreement by around twenty keen enthusiasts to lease, on a long-term basis, the site of the Keel Inn field. They also agreed and arranged the subscription fees, entrance to races (known as *legers*) and the exact mile point from the centre of a marked circle known as the *paddock*.

Pigeon lofts were usually placed on the perimeter of the paddock and the pigeons registered by a numbered ring on their leg. Two trusted members were elected as timekeepers and two synchronized watches were used. On leger days, one timekeeper stayed at the paddock, the other timekeeper was a mile away with the trainers and the pigeons to be raced. At an agreed time, the timekeeper told the trainer to release the first pigeon. In sequence, the birds were released every two minutes. Meanwhile, at the paddock, the owner and timekeeper waited at an expected time for the released birds. As soon as a bird touched down, "Let" was shouted, the watch stopped and the time recorded. This was all very frenetic as the next bird was due within three minutes. The shortest time recorded was the winner of the leger.

The mile release points were taken from the Ordnance map and maybe from a former Honeywell pigeon club. These mile places from the cardinal points of the compass formed a circle around the Honeywell paddock. These places were: Shaw Lane pumps (West); the Stump (East); 32 Steps (North) and L.M.S. railway viaduct (South) known as Wood Corner or Bobbin Mill. Others included the old

97

workhouse, now Pogmoor Road, and the site of a worked-out colliery known as Crakes pit on the Wakefield/Rotherham Road.

The Honeywell Club became a main attraction for all mile-racing pigeon men as many of their clubs were disbanded e.g. Worsbro' Common, Kingstone and Lundwood. The club lasted for around fourteen years and was then disbanded due to the clearance of the many terraced properties and the Keel Field for re-development.

THE 'OLD WHITE 'UN' AND 'MAD PAB'
Allan Williamson

Ellis Wilde came to live in the Honeywell area as a young man. A certain young lady called Dolly Howarth caught his eye and they married in the 1940's. He was interested in many outdoor sports, as many miners were. For many years his greatest sport was racing pigeons. He became a leading member of the Honeywell *paddock* along with his friend Ernest (aka Stinger) Greasley. As the Worsbro' Common *miler* club was in decline, they bought a white pigeon from Arthur Donohoe (aka Jie Dunnhoo) who had lived most of his life in Union Street. Jie had great experience in miler racing as he was an apprentice trainer for his father's birds, and recognised that the pigeon had great potential; he had already won many races when Ernest and Ellis bought him. By this time he was known as the 'Old White 'Un.' Jie joined the partnership as adviser and chief planner of strategy. Throughout his racing career the 'Old White 'Un' was a force to be reckoned with, winning practically every race and scooping up prize money. Eventually he was retired and Ellis kept him as a stock bird.

Meanwhile, Jie noted another pigeon with potential and persuaded Ellis and Stinger to purchase him for £1. This pigeon looked ungainly and according to the trio was big and daft, but just maybe could be great, if it responded to intensive training. They called it the 'Mad Pab,' because it wheeled around at first, instead of flying straight, but its speed in flight made up for the seconds lost. The 'Mad Pab' became outstanding, winning all his races and beating off challengers. He produced an offspring the image of himself called 'Cutneck,' the name given to him after a collision with telephone wires. Ellis saved his life by inserting sixteen stitches of cotton to staunch the heavy bleeding. Many would have culled him, but 'Cutneck' recovered and went on to win many races, but his racing career was short lived as racing ceased at the Honeywell paddock in the early 60's.

The 'Old White 'Un' was revered and lived on a couple of years, then vanished in mysterious circumstances. It was found dead two years later in an old drain in a nearby allotment, identified by his metal leg ring, possibly a victim of a domestic cat. The 'Mad Pab' was sold off along with other stock to other fanciers, although Ellis kept two pairs of his strain. When the paddock disbanded, a number of their members moved to a new site at the Royal Arms on Wakefield Road.

HONEYWELL BOXING CLUB
Roy Marsden

In 1953 I was fourteen, had a friend called Brian Fairclough, and we joined the boxing club at the rear of the Honeywell Public House. It was run as far as we were concerned by Jack Brownlie (snr), and his sons Jack and Terry were both members of that club. Both Brian and I travelled from Dodworth to train and be taught how to box at the club. I don't know just how many members there were, as we only went twice a week. There were about twelve to fourteen training when we trained. It was very clean and the older boxers were very good to us, and trained us how to look after ourselves.

We tried once or twice to get a drink from the pub, but we failed. We did once get a drink (brown in colour) but it was Angostura Bitters. It was horrible, so we didn't try again. This part of my life put me in good stead for the life I have had up to now, so thanks to all involved.

HOW THE WORLD FERRET-LEGGING CHAMPION WAS
Don Booker MBE

What a strange sight. There in a Honeywell allotment was a chap with his trouser bottoms tucked into his socks and his hands down his trouser top.

He was stood outside his cedar wood shed, a stove sending out black smoke and lots of junk around. There appeared to be movement down the trouser legs.

I leaned on his gate and shouted to ask if he was alright. "Ay, lad. I'm ok. I'm just training" was his reply. "Training for what?" I asked. "I'm the king of the ferret-leggers. I'm Reg Mellor." So that was Reg Mellor who had worked in the nearby nail factory and graduated to be security man at a warehouse, but spent his spare time in a shed with his ferrets.

He told me that his sport didn't allow jockstraps or underpants - and tight trousers made his act impossible. It was a rare way to strike-up a friendship with the sixty-eight year old champion, but I love characters and Reg was certainly that.

He was dapper, always wore a suit, and used Brylcream on his hair and wax on his military-style moustache.

Reg had his trousers around his ankles more than he had them under his belt, but his great skill was keeping ferrets down his trousers. He established a world record by keeping them down for more than five hours at the Holmfirth Country Show. He was still there when the spectators had gone home and the promoters were dismantling the stage.

When he tried to get that feat recorded in the famous Guinness Book of Records, the publisher refused – they said the sport was too dangerous.

I introduced Reg to the world, at a Barnsley Nights event held at the Ardsley House Hotel, in aid of The Northern Group of Motoring Writers. It was to promote the town and it's personalities like Ashley Jackson, Stan Richards, Skinner Normanton, Dickie Bird and musician Anastasia Micklethwaite.

Photographer Stan Bulmer collected Reg and his three ferrets, which were in a canvas bag, to bring him to the hotel. During dinner, there was a call for a car to be moved from the hotel entrance. It was Stan's Ford. When he went to move it, he was attacked by the ferrets who had managed to escape from their bags. Re-captured by Reg, they performed well down his trousers and did not climb into the hotel roof, which I had feared might happen.

Down the M1 we went, with the ferrets in a plywood box. We were on the way to Leeds to make a television film. With just two miles to go, one popped out of the box and I had to make an emergency stop. As expected, a police car with flashing lights soon stopped ahead. The officer approached, but I could not open the window and pointed to the ferret sat on top of the fascia; Reg grabbed it, put it back in the box and placed both feet on top; to our relief, the police officer waved us away.

Reg went on a tour of the UK and even a tour of Australia, appearing on television shows. Unfortunately he later developed heart problems and died aged seventy-six years.

My own memory of Reg is a stuffed ferret, which had died from breathing problems. It carried a plaque with the inscription; "To Don Booker for promoting ferret-legging."

Reg Mellor, fourth from right, at Barnsley Night at Ardsley House Hotel. Holding stuffed ferret is Freda Parkinson, mother of Sir Michael Parkinson. Others include Ashley Jackson, Anastasia Micklethwaite, 'Skinner' Normanton and Emmerdale star, Stan Richards.

On Don's retirement, presenting his stuffed Ferret, Syd, to Sir Nicholas Hewitt, Chairman of the Barnsley Chronicle, for safe keeping in the board room.

LIFE AT THE HONEYWELL INN
Doris Gosling

My father and mother moved to the Honeywell Inn in 1929. Previously, they were at the Woodman Inn at Ardsley. The Honeywell was a Barnsley Brewery House and the Woodman was a Clarkson House.

I remember we had to stay for the night with an aunt, as my parents had to stay at the Woodman to open up next morning, before going on to the Honeywell to do the same there.

I had my fifth birthday at the Honeywell.

Beckett Street Infants was my first school and I remember breaking my arm and having to have an operation. Next I went to Eldon Street Junior School. Mr. Foudeir was the headmaster and Mrs Spooner was my form teacher. My next school was Raley, where Mrs Chambers was headmistress and Mr. Bird was in charge of the boys. Girls and boys were kept separate in those days. Raley School had its own swimming baths and I believe it was the only school around at the time with this facility. It also had a cottage where girls were taught cookery and housekeeping. Raley also boasted a kiln, so we were able to have lessons in pottery making.

My mother always made soup, so on Saturday mornings my sister and I had to go to Brady Webster's in town for the ingredients. On Monday, after we finished school, we went to butcher Smith's at the end of Honeywell Street, to get the meat – a sheep's head! My mother made the soup and sold it on Friday; it was very popular.

A cobbler had his shop on the other corner of Honeywell Street, and did a good trade in 'clog irons' for the miners. The Misses Nock, had the post office. They also sold sweets and stationery.

When we first got to the Honeywell, we had a shire horse in the stable. It belonged to the coal dealer who lived two doors further on the street; I think his name was Mr. Dickson. My brother Jim kept pigeons in the loft above the stable and we kept our minerals in the remaining bit of the stable.

We had a big garage. In there was a bath, where the football team got changed. Over the top of the garage was the club room, which housed a billiard table and a boxing ring. My brother Jim also ran a cycling club from there. It was good to see all the lads setting off for a ride on their bikes on Sunday mornings.

Doris, with her dad and sisters

The A.R.P. (Air Raid Patrol) took over the club room during the Second World War; it had to close when an incendiary bomb went off during a demonstration, causing it to go through the floorboards. It was opened up again when the war ended and used for the celebration teas, although I remember dad saying that the entrance was unsafe, so when the celebrations were over it remained closed.

During the war we put on concerts, and the customers gave what money they could spare. This was collected and sent out to the local lads who were in the forces. A Roll of Honour was made up when the war ended and hung in the tap room.

Christmas was nice at the Honeywell Inn; we had a Christmas tree in the kitchen and trimmed up all the rooms. The Carol Singers used to come at midnight following a tradition of letting Christmas in; they always got a good collection because all the family were home to celebrate with us. My mother always bought a box of tangerines plus apples, mince pies and Christmas cake. Sadly my mother died in April 1937, but dad continued as landlord and we stayed on at the pub until 1954. I left school at fourteen and worked from home until the war started in 1939.

My two brothers were called up during the war; one joined the Air Force and one the Army; I also had a brother-in-law in the Navy. Another brother worked at Davy Browns. My sister, Dorothy, was sent to Thorpe Arch Ammunitions Factory. I remember her skin turned yellow, from the powder she used to fill the shells. She got married when her boyfriend Allan came home on leave. My other sister, Mary, married Tom Phillips and they and their daughter Mary, also lived at the Honeywell Inn with my father and me. We regarded our family very fortunate; they all returned home safe and sound.

We hadn't heard from the brother who was in the 8th Army, for almost a year. On Christmas Eve, my sister Mary and I were walking up Eldon Street, when we saw this soldier coming towards us. I remember saying to her, "This looks like our Jim," and it was him; imagine our surprise! We had a really good time that Christmas. He told us the ship that was bringing the soldiers home was attacked, so they had to dock in Malta for repairs.

Trips were organised from the pub during the war. The ladies went to Doncaster Races and the men went to the races at York. The ladies also went on pantomime trips to Leeds, Sheffield and Bradford.

When the war came to an end, we had lots of street parties. I remember staying up all night trimming the place and putting flags up in the street, and the men lit a big bonfire in the road. I think it was Blackett Mason, that got a big drum from somewhere, and he played it for so long, he went right through it. We held a parade with all of us in fancy dress. I was dressed in beer labels. Our Mary had on a captains' outfit, and Dorothy was a clown. We had great fun.

When we left the Honeywell Inn in 1954, my father was given a barometer, as he had been the treasurer for the B.D.L.V.A. (Barnsley and District License Victuallers Association), 1951 – 54.

'End of the War' Fancy Dress Celebration

THE QUEENS SILVER JUBILEE
Katherine Symcox

The residents of Honeywell Grove decided to hold a street party to commemorate our Queen's Silver Jubilee. For weeks before, we had raffles, coffee mornings, material sales etc; to generate the funds needed to make it a day for our children to remember. We made bunting for the street and each house decorated its windows with red, white and blue. We wanted to hold the party on the road but had a back-up plan (in case of bad weather), and hired Beckett Street school. By lunchtime on the day clouds gathered and so we did have the tea in the school.

A fancy hat competition was held with all the children getting a prize. We had Barnsley Music Band and a magician came to entertain us. All ages joined in and everybody had a good time.

Children of Honeywell,' Silver Jubilee Celebrations 1977'

Katherine Symcox and friends celebrate,' Queen's Silver Jubilee 1977'

BEER-OFF SHOP
Dee Williamson

In the 1940's, Mrs Rivers kept the shop at the corner of Old Mill Lane and Honeywell Street (now known as Dot's shop). It wasn't very large, had gaslight and rotten floorboards, and was known as the '*beer-off*' shop, where you could buy draught beer only in licensed hours. It wasn't like the other general dealers because of keeping to licensed hours opening of 11 a.m. to 2 p.m. and 6 p.m. to 10 p.m. Mrs Rivers also sold snuff and many 'over-the-counter' medicines.

Some of the older women in John Edward Street never patronized the pubs but stayed at home to look after the kids. No baby-sitters or child-minders for the working class in those days. Their drink was taken at home. Often I was sent to Mrs River's shop or the '*out sales*' of the Honeywell Inn, to get beer or bottles of stout, and snuff, for two women in particular. I would be aged about ten or eleven years old. Mrs Rivers would never serve draught or bottled beer to kids unless they had a note from an adult. A screwed top bottle was concealed in a shopping bag. Mrs Rivers would then draw the pumped beer into a measuring jug and then funnelled the beer into the bottle. After the cap had been screwed on, a printed gummed label was placed over it with the warning words, "Don't break the seal." Carefully, the bottle was placed back into the bag. For this errand I was given 2d (worth 1p today). Back in those times compared with today, Social Services would have had a field day.

LIFE IN THE 50's AND 60's
Brenda Marsden (nee Frost)

We lived in Honeywell Lane in a two up, two down house. There were five of us, three girls and my mum and dad. My dad worked in the mines. We never seemed to have any money but we got by, but only just. I know my mum and the lady next door went to jumble sales.

Alfred & Dorothy Frost

My dad loved to go fishing down on the canal. I used to take him sandwiches as he was there nearly all day, and we used to have a few pike for tea. My dad loved to cook the Sunday dinner. I used to go to Pickersgill's shop in Honeywell Street at 12 o'clock for his beer – three gills and a pint, in a bag to carry it home. They used to serve children then. He would have it with his dinner, and then go to bed while Mum washed the pots and pans up.

We played cards a lot before the television came along. But later we would all sit in the dark and watch the television together, just the fire glow and the light from the television.

There were long walks along the canal with Mum, Dad, my sisters, my aunties and uncles and their families, then picnics, fishing, and going to New Lodge over the waterfall and through the woods. My grandma and granddad lived in Well View in Honeywell. Granddad had the field and he had pigs, one called Bessie. I loved going into the place where he did the pigswill – it smelt lovely to me. He was a gardener and did people's home gardens. I used to go to my grandma's on a Saturday morning to clean the outside toilet and steps; she gave me two shillings and sixpence, which was a lot of money to me.

I went to Eldon Street School and then on to Raley School, but didn't enjoy my early years; I was off a lot as I was always poorly. I remember Mrs Trigg in the last years at Eldon Street; she was rather strict but I loved to listen to her reading stories.

I loved my time at Raley; I only lived five minutes from the school, but because I waited for my mates to call, we were always on the last push. Mr. Shaw was one of my favourites and I remember having a part in a play. I never thought I would love cookery and sewing, but I did, and I remember going down to the playing fields behind the Tolgate pub on sports days. I never had swimming lessons till I went to Raley; we were lucky as there was a pool there.

I will always remember going down to farmer Wright's field in the Honeywell Grove area and playing cricket or rounders; there were always loads of us, always sunny days. Another game we played was skipping; my mum and the lady next door (Mrs Barraclough) would turn a big rope and we all joined in. Then we played *bumps*, as we called them, throwing two balls on the wall outside our house on Honeywell Lane. Another game was *sticks*; we put three sticks with one on top like a cricket stump up the side of a wall, and in turns tried to knock the top stick off. When you did, you had to try to get them back up again. There were two teams, the first to get them back up again were the winners. I loved this game .... memories!

My best friend was called Elaine who was six months older than me. We went everywhere together. We went to Eldon Street School together, but in secondary school, Elaine went to Longcar and I went to Raley.

We went on walks on Sundays, as there wasn't much else to do in the 50's, and we nearly always ended up in Wilthorpe Park, then on to Tinkers Pond and the Thirty-Two Steps. We used to laugh a lot, Elaine and me. We went to each other's houses and one year we went on holiday with her mum and dad to Blackpool. Then one year she came with me and my family to Cleethorpes. Exotic places eh? Her dad would say funny things to us; he called us "Wait a Minute" and "Half a Mo." We drifted apart as we got older; different jobs brought new friends but we still keep in touch with Christmas and birthday cards. Elaine was my first friend, so I think you always remember your first and best friend.

My most memorable teenage years are of course the late 50's and the 60's; the most important person was my idol, Cliff Richard. My friends at Raley school were all fans of his too. We went to see him at Sheffield, twice. I did the booking through Wilson Peck in Sheffield. We all went on the train and screamed our heads off.

Brenda and Susan Frost

We all met up at one another's houses to play music; my mum and dad didn't mind as long as we behaved ourselves, which we did in those days. We used to go to the Y.M.C.A. and Barnsley baths to dance; the 'George's' was popular too.

The 60's were magical!

"THE WAY WE WERE"
Trevor Carr

Barnsley, back in the 1950's/60's, was a wonderful place to be, not least for the entertainment it provided. To be a young person in the sixteen to twenty-four year age group at that time was nothing less than marvellous. In my opinion we had everything. Barnsley was known all over England, as the place to be for a good night out. Even the older mature person could enjoy singing and dancing for free, in almost every pub either in town or on the outskirts.

Dress code in the fifties was very stylish, for both men and women. If you wanted to be very smart, it was a mohair silk tailored suit, with a fabulous shirt and tie for the men, and beautiful dance gowns for the ladies. On a more casual basis, the men still wore a tailored suit, sometimes with a waistcoat, and leather patent shoes. Women always wore beautiful feminine dresses or a very smart skirt and blouse.

The men would congregate at weekends, early in the evening, either in The Honeywell Inn or The Keel Inn, before making their way up into town. Once there we would separate and go our various ways, depending on what we planned to do that evening. Some of the places locally, offered live entertainment with a band for dancing and singing. At least three or four times a week we went to: the Wine Shades run by Tommy Fisher, the Corner Pin had a trio, the White Hart in Peel Square, the Globe Hotel, the Duke of York with Bob Roper, Manor Castle, The Old Warrior in Sheffield Road with Stan Richards and his Melody Maniacs, Coach and Horses, Theatre Royal, Vine Tavern (Music House), plus many more. Quite often, appearing somewhere in town, were radio stars like Joseph Locke, Old Mother Riley and Frank Randal. If you wanted to go a bit further afield, your choice might be: the Friendship in Gawber, Lundwood Hotel, The Cricketers Arms or Staincross Hotel, all offering first class entertainment.

If you fancied a spot of dancing, there was nowhere better than Barnsley. It boasted many dance halls, where you could dance the night away to the big band sounds of the day, with the likes of Joe Loss and his Orchestra, and The Ambassadors which were a fifteen-piece band, plus many more.

Dance halls included: the Drill Hall on Eastgate and The Cuban, with Eric Drake and his band. Many a 'works do' was held at the Three Cranes Hotel, which boasted two floors, one of which was a specially sprung one, which made dancing a delight. It helped you to get the rhythm. The Geoff Haigh Orchestra were regular players there. The Arcadian Hall with resident band, the Ambassadors, was another wonderful venue for dancing; so were The Georges and Barnsley Baths, where the pool was covered over in summertime, with a very springy dance floor. Top name bands were a regular feature playing this venue and dancing took place three times a week. Open for dancing six nights a week, was the 'Gym' situated on Dodworth Road; a carnival night was held there every month.

Another option to consider for your night out was the cinema. If this was your preference, then you had an extensive choice. We had quite a few picture palaces in the town centre alone. The Empire, on Eldon Street, The Ritz on Peel Street with Trevor Willets at the organ, Globe Cinema on New Street, the Pavilion at the town end, Princess on Racecommon Road and up Sheffield Road on Britannia Street was The Star, affectionately known as the Bugs Hut. The Alhambra Theatre was another great cinema. It had four floors, so it held a good number of people, and seat prices depended on which floor you chose. The *Gods* at the top being the cheapest. Just outside of town there was the Savoy at Lundwood, and also a cinema at Mapplewell, plus one in Wombwell and Penistone. The choice was endless. All of them showed a 'B' class movie first, then the feature film. In general, films were changed twice a week.

Youth Clubs in Barnsley were in abundance and provided activities and things to do for the younger end. Places like Y.M.C.A., Raley, Racecommon Road, Grove Street and Littleworth were all very popular Youth Clubs and well worth a visit.

Barnsley also claimed to have the biggest and best open air market in Europe. It was an outing not to be missed. Most men, if not working, strolled around the market place with their wives on Saturday. The market was held three times a week, on Wednesday, Friday and Saturday, although Saturday was without doubt the best one of all. People would come in bus loads to buy and be part of what was going on. Some of the traders, like Joe Edwards the Pot Man, were artists in action. He drew the crowds in every week, throwing his baskets of china dinner services around, so fast, you hardly had time to fear he was going to drop them, which to my knowledge he never did. He became a celebrity in his own right. Sailor Sid was another character and so was Albert Hirst, a Barnsley man, who became famous throughout the country for his Black Pudding and Pork Pies.

Barnsley feast week, the third week in August, was when the town evacuated to the seaside resort of their choice, which could be Blackpool, Bridlington, Scarborough, Filey or Cleethorpes. Some chose boarding houses, whilst others chose to go to Butlins Holiday camps. A lot of young people, myself included, would make for the delights on offer at Blackpool, where we might visit The Tower Ballroom or Winter Gardens, and enjoy dancing the night away to top artists, people like Joe Loss and his orchestra and Ted Heath. Appearing live at the Opera House were stars of TV and radio such as Frankie Lane, Johnny Ray, Lita Rosa, Dennis Lotis or Dickie Valentine, plus many more.

Barnsley Reds Football Club has always been very popular with every generation and the 1950's were no exception. Supporters were able to watch players like

Pat Kelly (goalkeeper) Danny Blanchflower, Tommy Taylor, Johnny Kelly, Arthur Kaye and Jimmy Baxter. Oakwell was up to its knees in star players and most went on to better things.

"MY CAREER IN ENTERTAINMENT"
Trevor Carr

My career in theatre and working men's clubs started in 1948, when I joined the Honeywell Glee Club along with my cousin Malcolm Bickerton, Chuck Phillips, Harriet Charlesworth and others. We entertained Senior Citizens in the local pubs and clubs around the area; one place in particular was the Salvation Army Station on Wellington Street, which is now a pub.

The first time I got up on my own was at the Pheasant Inn, Monk Bretton, when I sang 'Sonny Boy,' made famous by the late Al Jolson. It went down well with the crowd and everything was going fine until about 9 p.m. when in walked two Honeywell lads, Walter Wright and Tom Brown. They were both nineteen/twenty years old and because I was only fifteen years old at the time, I was sure they would tell my mother they had seen me in the pub. They agreed not to tell on me if I would go with them the following night, to the Friendship Inn, Gawber, where they entered me in the talent show which was held there. I subsequently won and continued to do so, many times in the following years.

One Sunday night I was booked to sing at the Green House, in John Street, Barnsley (Marquis of Granby), and did so for the princely sum of thirty shillings, which was great for a fifteen year old lad, on haulage, working down the pit and usually earning fifty-four shillings for a five-day week.

After this, I began entering the bigger talent shows like the ones held at the Ritz cinema on Peel Street which held 2,500 people, and the Theatre Royal on Wellington Street. I appeared on the Peter Webster Show, Central Pier, Blackpool.

By now it was 1951/52, and I was offered a regular spot at the Baths Hall in Barnsley, three or four nights a week for dancing; what an experience. After a couple of years doing this, I was longing to get back into the pubs and clubs that were very popular, and scattered all over town and the outlying district. I achieved

111

this in the following years, again doing the night club circuit, travelling as far as York and Manchester.

In 1959 I met my future wife Maureen, who accompanied me, travelling around England, to venues from coast to coast. One night, and after a lot of coaxing, she plucked up the courage to join me on stage, and we sang a duet, and the audience loved it. From then on, there was no stopping us. We were in demand all over the country - South Wales, Scotland and around the North east, singing under the name of 'Steve Jackson and Sunny Brown.'

In 1963, we were joined by Stan Richards (Seth Armstrong in Emmerdale) who at the time was a local Comic and Pianist and this partnership lasted seven or eight years, and took us to the South Yorkshire Command Performance, which was held at the New Road Club, in the summer of 1966. In the summer of 1969, we appeared at the Princess Theatre, Torquay alongside Frank Ifield. Although we were booked up solid for the next two years, the partnership ended on New Years Eve 1969.

My wife Maureen and I then joined up with Alan Harvey (piano) and Terry Clayton (drums), calling ourselves 'The Four Royals,' and played two shows at the City Hall Sheffield. Every Christmas Eve we had a standard booking at the Swaithe Club; Darfield on Boxing Day, and New Road, Staincross on New Year's Eve. These bookings lasted for years.

Our personal friends throughout these years were people like, Dickie Valentine, Bob Monkhouse, Charlie Williams, Paul Shane, Dukes and Lee and Tony Christie. Altogether we played a total of 4,000 engagements.

'The Four Royals'

One of the many fancy dress parties at a local pub

'Honeywell Ladies' enjoy a bus trip

Local people enjoying a night out

Andy Phillips

HONEY WELL COLLIERY
E Phillips

Honeywell, during the1700's, consisted of nothing more than a collection of agricultural fields, bound by Smithies Lane to the North, Eldon Street to the South, the River Dearne to the East, and Cockerham Lane to the West. There was only one other lane between Eldon Street and Smithies Lane, and that was Honeywell Lane, which led solely to the water well which gave the lane its name, and was to become the name of the whole area as we know it today. All this can be seen on the Ordnance Survey map of 1855.

There was no real change in the area until the Honey Well Colliery was established in the early 1800's. This was also named after the well, probably due to its close proximity. The colliery was established by the Thorp family who were the owners of a number of collieries in the area, namely Gawber New Colliery and North Gawber to mention but two. Gawber New Colliery was sited between Honeywell Lane and Smithies Lane, alongside the canal, as can also be seen on the map of 1855, page 118.

The Honey Well Colliery may have been a reasonably safe and productive mine; reasonably safe because there were no explosions or multiple deaths to be found in the records. Of course there would have been accidents, and in all probability the last one on the 21st of February 1863, being that of a twenty-two year old Gawber man, Mr. Wilson. He was working as a "hanger on" at the bottom of the shaft, when hit by a 14lb lump of coal, which fell the depth of the shaft, killing him instantly (information taken from the Barnsley Chronicle 150th Anniversary supplement, 29th February, 2008).

There is no documented information available for the Honey Well colliery, for example the number of workers or production figures. It ceased production in 1863, the advert being placed in the Barnsley Chronicle on the 14th November, 1863, for the sale of valuable colliery plant, by Mr George Brooke, on behalf of the executors of Mr Samuel Thorp (see advertisement).

It seems very strange that during the life of Honey Well Colliery, there were no dwellings to speak of. There were two houses, without numbers, recorded in1862. The next building to take place was of three houses in 1869, two of which were to become the Honeywell Inn, which would have been numbers 46 and 48 Honeywell Street. They were built by a Mr George Squires, who was also the first licensee of the Honeywell Inn, this also being in 1869. There were another two extensive phases of building, the first in 1871, numbers 55 to 89, and numbers 64 to 116 in 1876. There were other houses constructed after 1876, on which no details have been found to date.

There were other large employers in the Honeywell area, these being of course the Star Paper Mill and Redfearn Glass Works. The Dearne Paper Mill being its first name, and having been built on the site of the Old Mill Bleach Works, around 1870, it then became The Yorkshire Paper Mill, later to become the Star Paper Mill. Sadly it closed in 1981, with the loss of over 300 jobs. Redfearn Brothers Ltd. was formed in 1910 as a private company, which had previously been run by the Redfearn family since 1862, the original factory being Old Mill Works, Harborough Hills. A new factory was built at Monk Bretton in 1947.

SALE BY MR. GEORGE BROOKE.

TO COLLIERY PROPRIETORS, BROKERS, ENGINEERS, &c.
SALE OF VALUABLE COLLIERY PLANT AND OTHER UTENSILS, &c.
At the HONEY WELL COLLIERY, Barnsley,
(BELONGING TO THE EXECUTORS OF SAMUEL THORPE).

MR. GEORGE BROOKE will SELL by AUCTION, on the premises, on Wednesday, the 25th day of November, 1863, at Eleven o'clock precisely, a valuable Horizontal ENGINE, WEIGHING MACHINE PLANT, and UTENSILS, at the Honey Well Colliery, Barnsley, including :—an excellent Five Ton Weighing Machine ; Horizontal High-pressure Engine, Eight-horse power, very useful and in capital condition, with Drum &c. ; Boatman's Lobby, Walling Stones, Wood Framing, Jack Head Clack Piece, &c., Two Brake Wheels and Frames, Capstan Spears and Spear Plates and Bolts, a quantity of Ashlar Stone, 14 Coal Waggons, hold 2½ Tons. 3ft. 8½ in. gauge in good repair ; Two Coal Tipplers, Sinking Head Gear, with everything complete ; Two running Carriages ; Slide Windbore, 13 inches diameter, 11 feet slide, Metal Glands, &c., (cost £40) ; One Metal Working Barrel, 12 inches diameter, with Clack Piece, &c. ; Two good Laundry Boxes, Wood Centres, &c. ; Barrel and Wheel for Crab, &c. ; a very good Gin, almost new, with Head Gear, and in capital condition ; Two Bean Crushers (new), made by Clay, Stennard Iron Works, Wakefield; large Metal Cistern, 7 feet square ; 100 Yards of 3 inch Metal Pipes, 9ft. lengths, bored and turned ; Metal Drum Shaft, Two Metal Pillars, Pumping Shaft and Wheel, Tin Oil Lamps, and good Iron Sinking Corves.

At the Old Gawber Colliery :—large Brick Engine House, and 85 Tons of good Ashlar and Building Stone, will be sold, and many other valuable articles. 6 inch Working Barrel, Clack Piece with Quadrant.

The sale will commence precisely a Eleven o'clock.

The Plant, &c., may be viewed by application on the premises.

Honey Well Colliery: advertisement of sale of plant, etc., from the Barnsley Chronicle newspaper, 14.11.1863.

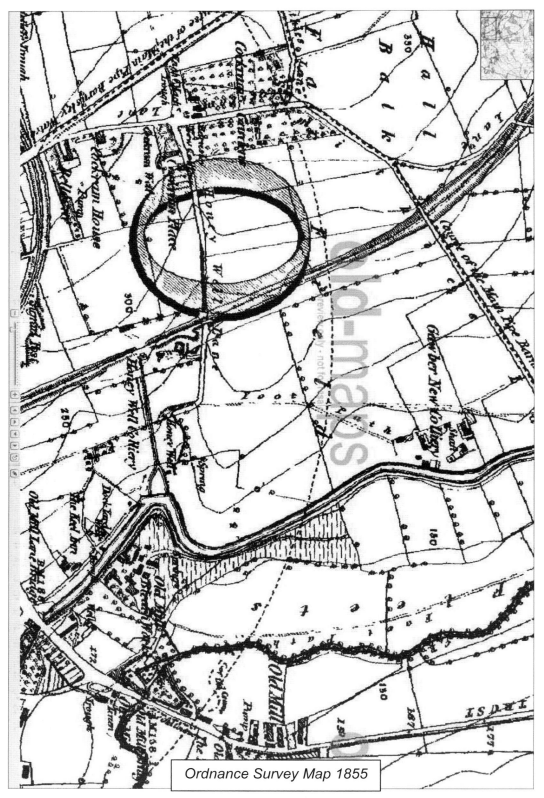

Ordnance Survey Map 1855

1984 – MINERS' STRIKE
Julie Johnson

We moved to Honeywell in June 1984 shortly after the beginning of the Miners' Strike. It officially began on 12th March of that year. My two boys were aged eighteen months and three years at the time. My husband was employed at North Gawber Colliery in Mapplewell, and had been there for several years. Our move to Honeywell came with mixed feelings of excitement at the prospect of moving to a new home and area, together with the uncertainty that being on strike brings.

Margaret Thatcher's Conservative government at the time had decided on a national pit closure programme, and had already stock-piled massive amounts of coal to power stations up and down the country ready for a long campaign ahead. She had brought in an American man called Ian Macgregor to carry out her vision – and so the game began!

News bulletins every day on TV became compelling viewing. The strike brought about a cocktail of feelings and behaviour as the strike took its hold over Britain. Whatever people's feelings were outside the industry, miners felt they had a cause worth fighting for, their jobs and livelihoods.

As the strike was taking hold, the hot summer arrived. Picket lines were held at the entrance to every pit up and down the country and violent clashes broke out when those wanting to return to work and break the strike tried to enter on coaches provided by British Coal. Scabs, as strike breakers were called, were ostracized within their communities and hated by their colleagues. It also broke families apart. Many clashes took place with police officers on picket duty, some said to be flashing their wage slips showing money they had earned working overtime during the conflict. Some miners died for their struggle.

There was no strike pay throughout, and families tried to survive on very little money, which often didn't even cover food bills, after deductions of £1 or £2 per month for mortgage, gas, electric and insurances. The telephone line was disconnected. Single men didn't receive anything and were only able to survive by receiving small amounts for picket duty or from their families and friends. We received help through food parcels now and again from donations given by the general public who were in support of our cause. We also had milk tokens, which we gave to our local milkman in payment of his daily deliveries, clothing and shoe tokens from the council to exchange for clothes and footwear for the children, which we took to a building on Pitt Street. Our families were a great support during this time, giving us carrier bags of food, for which we shall be eternally grateful. On days when we struggled, we went to the soup kitchens at the top of the Civic Hall in Barnsley where we ate a hearty dinner. However grateful, we often wondered how it had come to this.

As time passed and the weather was getting cold, my husband went over to the Willow (Willow Bank) to dig for coal and collect wood to keep the fire going. Christmas sort of came and went without any fuss as we couldn't afford to buy anything for the kids or anyone else, but our family rallied around and bought them extra presents so they wouldn't feel left out.

By 3rd March, 1985 the strike was over. Many pits had already closed, including North Gawber, through the pit review process because these were no longer seen as viable and the government was not willing to subsidise them any more. It was another couple of years before we managed to get back on our feet in terms of paying off the debt we had accrued i.e. mortgage and utility bill arrears etc. The redundancy we received went to pay off the debts and much needed items of clothes and furnishings for our new home.

The legacy: most of the pits closed in Britain with the exception of a few including the Selby coalfields in North Yorkshire, where some of the remaining miners moved to after the strike. The Nottinghamshire miners never came out on strike in support of their comrades in the Yorkshire and other coalfields. When I think about the strike I still remember those feelings of desperation, but also of the kindness of others. When I think about issues like global warming and how the coal industry must have contributed to its present state, perhaps it was all part of the big plan towards our survival that the pits closed. Would I go through it again – I think I would because if you believe in something that you think is right at the time, then yes, but knowing what I know now – no. Hindsight is a wonderful thing! These memories and feelings will never be forgotten and sit, like a bird on a perch, at the back of my mind.

REDFEARNS – 'THICK SMELLS OF GLASS'
Margaret Ferry

The glassworks were at the bottom of Harboro' Hills, and we lived in Denton Street, it was just across the road and down a little bit. It was a high building to a child and the blue doors were enormous. There were always men standing outside when you went past; it was a really strong smell of smoke, fire, and chemicals, I suppose. The men were all dressed in blue overalls and they were all dirty, but they waved and smiled, and they had glass bottles that they were drinking from – I presume it was water.

It smelled like a furnace when you went past, but they were always cheerful and they always smiled. Even in winter time, there would be men standing there, because it was so hot inside the factory. The canal went by the side of it; you could get down to the canal from the side of the glass factory. It was called Redfearns then. I don't think it was very big actually, but it seemed very big to a child.

THE NAIL SHOP
Doris Myers (nee Kemp)

I was born in 1923 and lived at 102 Honeywell Street, and started work at the *Nail 'Oyle* in 1937 aged fourteen. My way to work was down the snicket, past the Garden House, and through the Keel Field, passing the original pigeon club lofts and the caravans. The nail factory was located at the side of the canal bank, seventy or eighty yards from the Keel Inn. Our hours were 8 a.m. to 5 p.m. We had a dinner hour from 12 noon to 1 p.m. There were no canteen facilities, so like most local workers, we went home for dinner. The paper mill buzzer could be clearly heard.

The women wore brown smocks and the men were in overalls. My job was to use a machine which flattened the metal to make the head of a nail. These were then passed in bulk to another operator for the other end to be sharpened. I remember working with Billy Lowe, who lived in a terraced house by the canal bridge, and three sisters Annie, Lily and Norah Greasly who lived on Bridge Street. A chap called Alf was our boss, and the owner, Cyril Waring, worked alongside us. Hard dirty work, but at least we were employed.

ALL IN A DAY'S WORK
Bill Gaunt

On Tuesday afternoon I picked up Jack's tool bag and we got into George Wright's yellow van. George Wright was an electrician in Barnsley. Jack was his brother and worked for him. We started the day by driving down to Honeywell where Jack lived with his mother-in-law. He lived in Sarah Ann Street (I believe). We called at his house and picked up his *snap*. On the way to Notton, where we were to wire a light in a farm mistle.* He told me about living in the Honeywell Farm where his father farmed. It was demolished because it only had one door. Jack's father held the shooting rights to the Fleets lake, and during the winter on certain Sunday afternoons, they had shooting days.

*A mistle is an outdoor covered barn for cows with no sides.

"SHOPPING TRIP IS LIKE GOING HOME FOR THE OUTWINS"

(Taken from an article, by Kath Parkin (Memories), in the Barnsley Chronicle – 14th January 2000 edition, provided by Joyce Outwin)
Julie Johnson

When the Outwin family does their weekly shop at Asda, it's a bit like going home. On the site where the giant supermarket now stands, there used to be two houses, one of which was occupied by the Outwins. Where Asda staff car park now stands used to be their former back garden. Where the store's bacon counter now stands is where the family's house once stood and they have a bit of a joke about it.

Many years ago the land was owned by the Paper Mill, and Joyce Outwin's in-laws, Ivy and Frank Outwin, leased a house from the owners, where many of the Outwins and her own family worked.

Frank and Ivy's son Harry, and daughter Betty were born in the house; Tom in 1923 and Harry (Joyce's husband), in 1926. Both Joyce and Harry also lived in a house there until 1977, when the houses were pulled down. Harry and Tom worked at the mill for many years. Tom eventually emigrated to Auckland, New Zealand, until his death in 1997. The Paper Mill shut down in 1981.

'Outwin family' camping out, in Paper Mill Yard

HONEYWELL AND THE STAR PAPER MILL
Joyce Outwin

My in-laws, Frank and Ivy Outwin, went to live in the Star Paper Mill yard in 1925, and lived there for forty-one years until Frank's retirement in 1966. They had three children, Tom, Harry and Betty.

Tom was born in Eldon Street in 1924. Harry (my husband) was born in 1926 and Betty in 1930, both in the large old house in the mill yard. On one occasion, while Betty was going to school in Eldon Street, the mill chauffeur, George Kilner, knocked her down while she was crossing the road. She spent her fifth birthday in hospital.

Houses in the mill yard

Frank and Ivy lived there until they moved into number 7, one of the two new houses built in the mill yard. Later, Harry and I went to live in their house until we were told that the mill was to close, and in 1977 we went to live on the Grove. There were three other houses facing the Keel Inn, where the Hollingsworth and Batty families lived.

Harry Outwin, at work 'Paper Mill'

Originally, the houses in the mill yard only had electricity from Monday morning till noon on Saturday, because it was generated by the mill and when the mill closed down for the weekend, the electricity was switched off, and the houses had to use gas lighting. In 1952 - 1953 they updated all the houses in the yard, putting Town Electricity in. They also put lights in the yard because there hadn't been any, and dark nights were very eerie when you were going home, especially with the big stacks of pulp they used for making paper (the road going down to the Asda car park is the original road where they stacked the pulp). They also put water toilets in (they had been outside) and tiled the bathroom and kitchen. The two semis, numbers 7 and 9, were built on the site of a little white cottage which was pulled down to make way for them. When Frank and Ivy went to live in number 7, their big old house was also pulled down. The houses were on the spot where the Asda staff car park now stands.

I also remember that a railway ran at the back of the mill which delivered coal for the boilers, and then continued down Wakefield Road at the back of the houses. Barges on the canal also went round the mill, and there were caravans in the Keel field at the side of the Keel Inn.

Frank was a foreman. Tom, his first son, also worked at the mill before he went to work at the Grimsby branch of Star Paper Mills, and later in the 1950's, went to work at a paper mill in New Zealand. Harry worked on the railways as a fireman on the steam trains, and came back to the mill in the 1960's. He worked his way up to foreman and stayed there till the mill closed in 1981.

There were three fires in the mill yard in its lifetime, where the pulp had caught fire. No one was hurt. A more serious fire on 2nd September 1867 did a lot of damage.*

The mill also had a very good bowling green and sports ground where they held sports days for staff and their families. They also had fishing on the *fleets*, which still goes on today.

I also remember the shops in the area in those days - the hairdressing shop, Style Corner on Eldon Street, was once a cobblers shop. There was Albert Hirst the butcher, a bread shop, Post Office, paper shop, Megan's greengrocers, a barber shop and the Co-op was on the left-hand side. Beckett Street School was round the corner and at one time there was a dentist in Beckett Street.

When we moved to the Grove, there wasn't a proper road for a few years and the residents had to pay towards the cost of a new one. The fields at the side of Honeywell Place had a very large hole and a very large tree. Boys used to put a long rope up and swing from side to side, until one day around 1978, it broke and a boy was badly hurt.

One of three fires at the' Paper Mill'

The tree was sawn down and the hole filled in. I remember Mr. Marion, who was blind and well known, kept geese, a horse and a goat down on the gardens. Now, there are fancy flats there.

In the early hours of Monday, 2nd September 1867, the Star Paper Mill was destroyed by fire. A member of staff, who lived on the premises, discovered the fire and raised the alarm. The blaze was so fierce it could be seen for miles around, and the main four-storey building was completely destroyed. Fortunately, the finished paper stockrooms and engine house stood apart from the main building and were saved

LIFE IN THE PAPER MILL YARD
Betty Birks (nee Hollingwoth)

Barges came on the canal bringing coal for the boilers. It was stored until required. They were unloaded near the canal bridge. There was a pipe that sucked up the coal, and it was then tipped near to the railway line, just opposite house number 7, Paper Mill yard. This house was occupied by Frank and Ivy Outwin. Frank worked at the Mill, and they had three children at that time: Betty aged about 2 years and Thomas and Harry, who also went on to work at the mill.

The houses in the Mill yard, like most of the terraces around, had outside earth toilets (closet). These were called 'Middens,' where ashes from the previous day's fire were thrown in, to cover whatever was in there. The dustmen came very early morning to empty them, by shovelling it out (what an awful job, I can't imagine that in today's world).

Playing on Barrels in Papermill Yard Harry and Charlotte Popplewell used to live at number 9; it was a little white cottage.

When we were kids, we used to run up and slide down the coal (muck stack as we used to call it). There were some metal barrels we played on and some wooden ones that had resin in, which was used in the paper making process.

Playing on Barrels, in the 'Paper Mill Yard'

When it came around to bonfire night, we were allowed to have an empty barrel, which was filled with the wood from other barrels. For obvious reasons, we couldn't have a fire in the yard, but my dad used to get some wood, and we took them to a friend's house. There, we had the best fire around because of the resin, some of which was still stuck in the barrel; it was always still burning the next morning.

The Mill Social Club organised outings for its workers' kids, 1951/52. We went to watch the pantomime at Bradford Alhambra Theatre; we were then given our tea and a present

Sometime in the early 1950's, house numbers 7 and 9 were demolished; the occupants were moved to new semi's that had been built for them. Later, during the 1980's, all the houses were pulled down.

The Star Paper Mill closed in 1981. .

Demolition of, 'Star Paper Mill' March 1987. (Tasker Trust)

Children's Bus Trip, to the 'Alhambra Theatre, Bradford'

STAR PAPER MILL
David Phillips

My first job when I left school was as a paint sprayer at a garage in town. I did enjoy that job, but things were hard for my mum, and I knew it would be a few years before my training would finish and I could start earning money. My uncle, Andrew Phillips, worked at the Star Paper Mill and subsequently got me a job there. I started work in 1959, and saw many changes happen around me during my first twelve months. I was put to work with the women in the *'sall,'* not a position to be taken lightly for a young lad of sixteen. The best day of the week, and one we all looked forward to was Friday; not only was it pay day but all the women brought sweets in for us lads.

One of the ladies I worked alongside was Rita England (Britton), now well known in her own right as the owner of 'Pollyanna,' an upmarket ladies boutique in the centre of town, and she did well for herself our Rita.

Breakfast at work was always *'jam haggies,'* which were basically a jam pastry, but they were very nice and a popular treat.

Eventually as I became more experienced, I was moved around the mill and got to work on most of the machines: the cutters in the *sall*, *reelers* in the machine house, and eventually on to the main machine house.

The main machines operated on steam, and if anything went wrong with them, all man power was needed for the repair. We used very large felts in the paper making process, and if a felt broke, the staff were allowed to take them home for their own use. When I first got married, my wife and I used the felts around the house, saving us money on under felt for the bedroom carpets, and lagging for the boiler; some people even had them as top blankets on cold winter nights. A bloke I knew, his wife made him a body warmer from one. They were even used in the garden for lining hanging baskets etc. The felts were a bonus to us when times were hard, and I don't know anyone who worked at the mill who did not use them if they got the chance.

We also used white cotton sacks at the mill, and when empty, we were allowed to take them home. These were very useful once they had been washed and dyed to your desired colour. They could then be used for curtains and other furnishings. There was a lot of recycling going off at the mill; I even made a nice standard lamp from the bobbins that came from the centre of the reels. After they had been varnished and fixed together, it looked good and everyone admired my handiwork.

The paper mill was a very hot place to work, especially in the machine house, when we needed to climb some steps to oversee the machines. They were so big, and checks were done periodically for faults on the paper coming through. As you can imagine, the higher you got, the hotter you became; sweat would pour out of us. The reel had also to be checked from the underside, because if a fault of some sort was not noticed, it would ruin the whole batch of paper, so it was someone's job to get underneath at intervals. This meant the big reels of paper were only inches from your face then (no health and safety). Whilst I only know this as hearsay (but I can imagine it is true), one man, whenever he went under the reels to do a check, frequently fell asleep because it was so hot and sweaty. On one particular day, his mate - if you can call him that - blew some powder dye under the machine. When he awoke and came out, he was yellow all over, and no matter how he tried he could not get it off.

A workmate, who lived alone, often did his laundry there. Not bothering to take his smelly socks home, he used to boil them along with his overalls, in a forty-five gallon drum of hot water and soda ash. Then he would jet them with steam before hanging them up to dry. Because it was so hot, a shower was made out of a bucket with holes punched in the bottom. A piece of felt was fastened up, and someone would hold a hosepipe in the bucket, over the top of whoever was getting washed. No-one needed to go home dirty and smelling of sweat. We had a few incidents with that one, as you can imagine, but that is another story.

There was a lot of static electricity about, which was caused by the friction of paper moving so fast. It didn't half make you jump at times. A safety wear steel toe-capped boots; because of the heavy work we did, it was necessary. One machine had a lever which we would put on with our foot; you could actually see the blue sparks flying quite high sometimes. A woman from another department used to come and take samples to be checked. If a particular person saw her arriving, he would run his hand along the paper. Then when she got very close, he would point at her asking what she wanted, knowing full well she would feel the charge. She soon learned to keep out of his way.

David and Gloria Phillips, trying out his new bike

The workers would always have a small bet on one of the horses on Grand National Day. This was known as a sweep. Nothing much was gambled, but ten pence was a lot of money in those days, and if you were lucky enough to be a winner, you felt you were really "in the money."

There was a foreman who always wore clogs. I don't think he ever *cottoned-on* to the fact they were noisy, and that if we happened to be doing something we ought not to do, like *acting about,* we knew he was coming because we heard him before we saw him.

If the machines were running well, and all was going smoothly, we were able to sit down and have a *cuppa,* using teabags with strings, which we hung up to dry in our locker so they could be used again. One foreman though, could not stand the thought of us doing nothing, so if we saw him coming, we automatically grabbed a brush; anything for a quiet life. Inevitably during these times, pranks were pulled on some poor unsuspecting bloke. I remember one time, a mate looking for his *snap*, which included some bananas. He found them hanging from the roof void. That evening, when it was time to go home, his bicycle was missing. He finally found it hanging up there with his bananas.

A friend on *nights* once spent quite a while during the shift carefully boring a hole through the bottom of his mate's tea mug. Then he fastened it to the bench. You can well imagine how the scene went, when his friend tried to pick it up.

As mentioned before, it was so very hot working in the machine shop; we drank a lot of water and tea. One friend lived in the mill yard. When he was on afternoon shift, his wife would go in all weathers to the Keel Inn or Prince of Wales to fetch a jug of beer, ready for when he had finished his work. It was not all fun and games though.

One bad spell was when I broke both my thumbs, causing me to be off work for weeks, and with two small children to feed and clothe, it was no joke. The job I was doing when I had my accident would not be allowed today, for health and safety reasons. Soon after this incident the procedure was changed. I remember a bloke who worked on the *reeler*. His rolls were always heavier by 200lbs; no-one could understand it, until someone at last realised he was weighing himself with the reels.

I enjoyed my time working at the paper mill. We had more good times than bad, and I made a lot of good friends. In all I stayed there fifteen years, before making my mind up to move on.

Two, of the paper making machines in operation, at the 'Star Paper Mill'

'Star Paper Mill' (Tasker Trust)

Elizabeth Carr, at work in the' Paper Mill'

'Star Paper Mills' 1890 workers.

'Star Paper Mills' ... (Tasker Trust)

Canteen, 'Star Paper Mill'

WORKING LIFE
Elaine Miller (nee Holmes)

When I was thirteen years old, I started work on the flower stall in Barnsley market; it was owned by Ron and Pat Smales, who also lived on Honeywell Grove. The job I had, meant I worked after school on Wednesday, and all day Saturday, and I loved it. My wages were half–a–crown (12 ½ p today) a week. Every Saturday morning, at 9.30 a.m., Ron would go and get us a bacon butty.

I left Longcar Central School on Friday, and started work the following Monday at Wilson's Fashion Shop, which was situated on Eldon Street. I worked as a cashier in the office upstairs. The money and tickets for items sold etc. came to us via a chute. I made out the receipts and then put it, along with any change, back into the chute. It was then sent back down to the customer. Mrs Widdowson was the Manageress. She was a very popular lady and I loved her.

The corridor upstairs used to overlook the market, and I can remember 'Joe Edwards' on his *pot stall,* throwing dinner and tea services up in the air and shouting "Who'll give me a bob (5p today) for the lot?"

I worked at Wilson's until I got married, and moved to Wakefield. I managed to get a transfer to another shop in the same chain, known as Graftons.

MY WORKING LIFE (1960-1966)
Brenda Marsden (nee Frost)

I started work as soon as I left Raley School at 15 years old. I went for an interview before I left in March (Easter). I was one of the lucky ones to have a job before leaving school. I started at Dawson Bro's at the top of North Eldon Street Arcade, a new shop. I wasn't there long though as the man in charge, my boss, wasn't very nice, so

Brenda and Susan Frost

I left and got a job at Butterfields & Massies. With living in Honeywell Lane, I used to walk it to work and back home every day, come rain or shine. I worked in the Linen Department – curtains and bedding. There were a lot of various

132

departments in store. We were rivals with the Co-op and seen as an upper class store in the 50's and 60's.

When we got to our job we had to clock into work first. We had a canteen where you could get a meal. At Christmas we always had a grotto for Father Christmas, down in the basement, where children came to see him and always got a gift.

We had Sales at various times in the year. We didn't have tills in the departments there; we had a system where you wrote a bill out, put the bill and money into a container, which went on a rail, up to the cashier in a separate department. They took the money and then sent the bill back with any change, and we gave the customer it back.

I enjoyed my job. When we finished work, we clocked off, and then went around the back. It was called George Yard, where we used to meet our boyfriends at the bottom of the yard, on a Saturday night. I made some good friends and had some good times. I was lucky there; I loved working there – in fact I stayed until 1966, just before my first son was born.

ELDON STREET NORTH
Katherine Symcox

In 1965 I came to live on Bridge Street which is only three or four minutes walk from Barnsley town centre and the market. However, at that time I could walk down Eldon Street North and pick up almost anything that a family might need from the many shops that were there. We had two greengrocers, two butchers, a confectioner, general store, barbers, hairdressers, draper, bookmaker, chiropodist, post office, newsagent and of course a branch of the Co-op. There were also two fish and chip shops, a watch repairer and cobbler.

All these businesses gave personal service, a cheery word, happy smile and sometimes even a chair to sit on whilst we waited to be served.

Today we go to Asda, Morrison's or Tesco and whilst it is convenient to shop in one place and be able to get everything in one go, it isn't as friendly, or green for the environment as it was then. Sometimes when you need only two or three things, you still come out with three carrier bags full. So I say "bring back the corner shop!"

'Redfearn' workers take a break

'Redfearn' Fitting Shop Workers 1937

'Redfearns' Accounts Office staff 1960, Allan Gothard, back row first left

'Redfearn' Cricket Team 1937

Unknown

FROM SMALL BEGINNINGS ......'KES'
David Bradley (aka Billy Casper)

I didn't grow up in the Honeywell neighbourhood – my *'home turf'* during the late 1950's and 60's was Athersley – yet this area played a significant role in shaping my early years.

Relocating to Smithies from Kingstone at the age of five, I found myself attending Burton Road Nursery and Junior School, rambling daily through the countryside with other youngsters and a parent, lost in imagination and chatter. At break time in the playground (beyond the World War Two air raid shelter), we'd watch steam trains shunting coal trucks back and forth along the line, occasionally crossing over Burton Road for a closer look at these monsters of the industrial age. Thomas the Tank Engine eat your heart out!

Many a summer's day was spent down at the Fleets, watching anglers land their catch on straining rods; or swinging over the River Dearne by means of a rope attached to an overhanging tree; or visiting the Old Star Paper Mill to 'ogle' their flame-raging furnaces; and when no-one was around, sneaking through the wire fence to play football on the Star Paper Mill pitch.

These were halcyon, albeit tough times; a child's world full of wonder without Text Messaging, Facebook and Twitter, when many families still had outside toilets, and rented *slot-coin operated* televisions, with programmes starting at four in the afternoon that would end with 'God Save The Queen' at midnight. This was also when youngsters like myself used to pay six old pence (2½ p) for a Saturday children's matinee at The Gaumont or ABC Cinema (Mighty Mouse was my favourite cartoon!), while Mam went shopping for groceries in what was known as the best open-air market in the country – that during Bank Holiday Feast week transformed into an humongous magical fun fair.

At the latter end of the 1960's, Barnsley rarely featured beyond its own borders regards social history, yet an event in the pipeline was being primed to turn an insular coal mining town into the talking point of the nation. A relatively unknown author from Hoyland, and two radical individuals in the BBC Drama Department, who had directed/produced several "Wednesday Plays," were to collaborate in making a feature film about a young boy from a dysfunctional family, whose work prospects, owing to a prejudiced educational system, are consigned to "factory fodder." The one redeeming grace is when he steals a Kestrel chick, and trains her like a true falconer. Many thought the plot line hardly presaged box office potential (no sex, no violence, plus a broad local dialect) and it was to be cast with unknowns: school kids, teachers, coalminers and local folk, plus stand-up artists playing the Working Men's Club circuit – all who had no experience of film making.

Over two hundred kids that had failed their Eleven Plus exams auditioned for cameo and classroom characters, with a selected few chosen to read for the coveted role of Billy Casper in the film 'KES.' Several days after the final audition, which was held at the now defunct Queens Hotel, I received a note from the director, Ken Loach inviting me to play the role of Billy.

Filming took place at various locations around Barnsley throughout the summer holidays, one of which is no longer there – John Edward Street (just off Honeywell Street). Back then there were no modern bungalows at the bottom end of John Edward Street; just coal-blackened terrace houses that curved up and connected with Honeywell Street above.

However, the cobbled archway where Billy back-tracks to check a discarded fag packet, in the background one can see Burton Road School (which still remains today) along with long gone metal work outbuildings.

' KES,' the film that put Barnsley on the map, is still a major influence on the fabric of our town and Britain's social history: documenting real life in a northern working class town, as well as being part of the educational syllabus not only nationwide, but also in other English speaking countries – inspiring stigmatised youngsters to challenge stereotyping, or a life with scant prospects.

We owe a great deal of thanks to the author Barry Hines, and director Ken Loach, who invested so much trust in a cast taken largely from the town community. I know they feel indebted to all that participated in 'KES' during those few short weeks in the summer of 1968.

A scene from 'Kes' – 'Billy' standing in the ginnel – with a view in the background over the Keel Field towards Burton Road and the School.

'Billy' running along John Edward Street in the film 'Kes' – both photographs courtesy of David Bradley (aka 'Billy Casper')

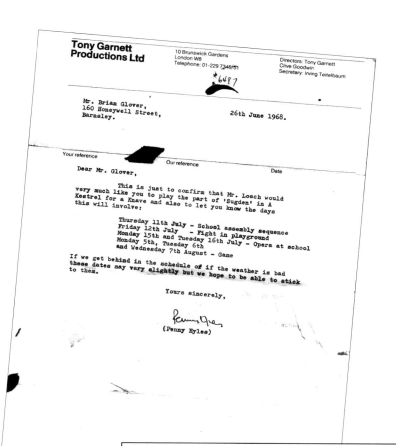

Tony Garnett Productions Ltd

10 Brunswick Gardens
London W8
Telephone: 01-229 7346/51

Directors: Tony Garnett
Clive Goodwin
Secretary: Irving Teitelbaum

*6487

Mr. Brian Glover,
160 Honeywell Street,
Barnsley.

26th June 1968.

Your reference

Our reference

Date

Dear Mr. Glover,

This is just to confirm that Mr. Loach would very much like you to play the part of 'Sugden' in A Kestrel for a Knave and also to let you know the days this will involve:

Thursday 11th July - School assembly sequence
Friday 12th July - Fight in playground
Monday 15th and Tuesday 16th July - Opera at school
Monday 5th, Tuesday 6th and Wednesday 7th August - Game

If we get behind in the schedule of if the weather is bad these dates may vary slightly but we hope to be able to stick to them.

Yours sincerely,

(Penny Eyles)

Registered office:
Nabarro, Nathanson and Co.
211 Piccadilly London W1

The letter from 'Mr Loach' offering Brian Glover, the part of 'Sugden' in the production of 'Kes'

Brian Glover third left, with other professional wrestlers Mick McManus, Jackie Pallo, Adrien Street, and others watching preview of 'Kes'

JOHN EDWARD STREET
Dee Williamson

John Edward Street consisted of two rows of terraced properties facing each other. Sarah Ann Street ran down an incline from Honeywell Street to the bottom of John Edward Street. Honeywell Street was known as the top street. Our name, John Edward Street, was sometimes called 'Low Aggers' by the kids, a derogatory name, so there was always rivalry between us as to who could have the best street party, biggest bonfire, best at street games etc.

One side of John Edward Street had even numbers and the opposite side – odd. All had communal back yards and outside toilets, which were shared by two families. The odd number side was longer than the even side, as between No.'s 3 and 7 there was a ginnel leading to the communal yard. From No. 9 to No. 21, another ginnel which lead to the Keel Field. Another five houses made up the rest of the street. All the properties were two up, two down, except for No's. 1,7,9,21 and 23 – which had three bedrooms because of the ginnels. The odd number properties also had cellars.

John Edward Street was used when Dai Bradley ran down the street in the film 'Kes' and paused in the ginnel between No. 21 and 23. All these properties were demolished in the late 60's. Brian Glover who starred in 'Kes', and also in the television series 'Porridge', lived in a bungalow on Honeywell Street and frequented the Honeywell Inn, but never mixed with the regulars. The Honeywell Community Centre now partly stands on the site where the properties of the old No. 12 to 20 John Edward Street would have been.

HOME SWEET HOME
Barbara and Robert Sharpe

We were on one of our usual walks round Willow Bank when we came across an empty bungalow. We did a quick walk around it, and thought what a big jump up from our terraced house to a detached bungalow. The lady next door saw us and asked us if we wanted to live down here. We said we would, at which she said 'If you would like to live round here, I am thinking of selling my bungalow. We took a look round and really loved it. Lots of land, good views, fairly modern – perfect. She gave us a cup of tea, we had a natter and took her phone number and her name (Mrs Butterfield) and she took ours. Our thoughts and discussions were quite extensive over the next week – excitement, anxiety – could we afford it? How much would she want for the bungalow? TWO WEEKS later, she rang us and said that she had decided to sell. We put our house up for sale and luckily it sold straight away.

We bought 27, Willow Bank in 1972 and brought up two boys there. Lovely memories.

FIRE AT A BARNSLEY GARAGE
Elaine Miller

'A fire at a Barnsley Garage was averted by the prompt action of two Barnsley men' (*Extract taken from the Barnsley Chronicle – date unknown*).

One night, Mr. Frank Christopherson of Rockingham Street, Barnsley, heard sounds suggesting a fire in the garage of Mr. Tom Roberts, a haulage contractor. He immediately informed the proprietor's daughter-in-law, who called for the Fire Service. An employee at the garage, Mr. George Holmes, was also informed, who upon entering the garage, found tyres of a lorry and tarpaulin burning. He drove the lorry outside and put out the flames using a hand extinguisher. The damage was slight but could have been far worse had the alarm not been raised as early as it had.

SMITHIES LANE FLOODING
John A. Thomson

Smithies Lane

Part of Smithies Lane and the bridge were rebuilt in the early 1970's. Whilst the repairs were taking place, the lane was closed for almost two years; however a temporary foot bridge was put in place.

During the demolition and construction of the new bridge, a plaque was found on the old bridge. The workers put it to one side intending to have it cleaned up before it was re-sited but vandals got hold of it and it got smashed. I was told by one of the men working on the bridge that he thought the date on the plaque was late 1700's.

Whenever it rained heavily, this stretch of the lane flooded and it was impossible to walk or drive on this stretch of road.

All this stopped once the road and bridge had been renewed, and remained like that until the heavy rains of 2007, when the floods came and once again the lane was closed for a short time.

Smithies Lane 2007

32 steps + shadow on frozen canal, about 1952 (Tasker Trust)

Skaters on the' Fleets' Christmas Morning, 1961. (Tasker Trust)

Swans on frozen canal (Tasker Trust)

Fishing, Barnsley Canal (Tasker Trust)

'John Edward Street' ready for demolition, (Tasker Trust)

'Honeywell Street' houses almost ready to be demolished (Tasker Trust)

"WE'LL BE GLAD TO SEE THEM GO"
Julie Johnson

(Taken from an article in the Barnsley Chronicle in 1976 before re-development of Honeywell Street, John Edward Street and Sarah Ann Street took place).

Ninety-one houses on Honeywell Street, John Edward Street and Sarah Ann Street, under a compulsory purchase order by Barnsley Council, will fall to the demolition squad to make way for the building of new houses.

Some comments at the time were: "They want pulling down. They are small, damp places – a lot of them have been empty for years. I'll be glad to see them go," said Mr. H. Green (64). Mrs. Brenda Utley (29) of Sarah Ann Street, said: "I couldn't be happier. The houses are damp, with paper hanging off the walls, and rats in the yard." Mrs. Janet Wright (26), also of Sarah Ann Street, feels just as strongly about the houses: "I have three children under five-years old, and they all sleep in the same bedroom as my husband and me, because their bedroom is too damp. The houses are so old that people have been born, lived and died here."

The following year, on Friday, 23rd September, 1977 another article appeared in the Barnsley Chronicle entitled: "Civic ceremony gives send-off to 'unique, exciting,' housing scheme," stating the houses and flats have been designed to exploit the natural slope of the ground, and provide distant views towards Monk Bretton, whilst retaining privacy and allowing the maximum amount of sunlight to enter the windows. The first turf on the £725,000 Phase I Honeywell Re-development Scheme was cut by Deputy Mayor, Councillor Frank Kaye. The Mayor, Councillor John Stanley, was presented with a silver trowel for the civic silver collection, by Mr. Maxwell Dernie, Managing Director of H. Dernie & Sons (Builders) Ltd., of Sheffield, the main contractor.

The Scheme provides for the construction of the first local authority split level houses in Barnsley. There will be forty of them and also thirty flats, on a steeply sloping site between Honeywell Street and Old Mill Lane, Barnsley. The first dwellings would be ready for occupation next June, and Phase II would be started immediately the first phase was completed.

'Honeywell Street' houses ready for demolition, the end of an era. (Tasker Trust)

Present at Tuesday's ceremony, as guests of the council, were disabled miner Mr. Ronald Cherryholme (52) and his wife, Lily, who will tenant one of the first specially designed and equipped dwellings for the disabled.

In response to the articles above, Gloria Hesford writes:

RESPONSE TO "WE'LL BE GLAD TO SEE THEM GO"

Whilst in the Barnsley archives looking through back copies of the Barnsley Chronicle 1976, I came across the article referred to in "We'll be glad to see them go" say the residents. It made me feel very sad, not that the houses were to be demolished because I could understand how the residents felt having lived in that kind of accommodation. I felt sad because the community we have been hearing about would inevitably be destroyed, along with the demolition of the houses.

We must remember that although these houses were now out of date and past their usefulness, there was a time when people were happy to call them home. Thinking back to my childhood, I know how fiercely proud my mum was of her home, although by today's standards we had very little.

Homemade rag rugs, were taken out and beaten every day, to get rid of dust and dirt, the front step was washed and donkey-stoned and woe betide anyone who stood on it. Wash days were very difficult because water first had to be boiled up in a *set-pot*, 'Dolly Blue' would need to be used to keep the whites bright; some things needed to be starched, which was another process - remember there were no washing machine's for most people, but still white nets hung at the windows and at mealtimes the table always had a clean cloth on it.

Because the community around you was all in the same boat so to speak, no one had more than anyone else, so they all looked out for each other. You could go to bed and not worry about making sure the door was locked; if you were having visitors and you had no bread, you nipped next door, for the proverbial cup of sugar. When you were ill or in trouble of any kind, folk gathered around; there was always someone to help. If there was bereavement, two ladies on the street could be relied on to 'lay the person out.' Even in childbirth it would be "go fetch Mrs. ….."

We have been told these stories by many of the people who lived in these houses, particularly during the war years and just after; those were years when you really had to pull together. This kind of housing made it easier to be neighbourly; there were no gardens just backyards. So as you can see by our cover-story pictures, people would get cups of tea and sit outside their front doors and watch the world go by.

Now we are all in our nice new semis or other modern homes, there is a lack of community spirit and people don't have the time to be neighbourly. Besides, now it is just not 'done.'

So although our standard of living is much better without these 'old houses,' and they did need to go, let's not forget what they once meant to some of us.

BIBLIOGRAPHY

Wilson, R, (1991) *Holy Wells and Spas of South Yorkshire* (Northern Arts).